O BY GEORGE BURNS

WISD

AL

Hou
Dr. E

WISDOM
OF THE 90S

George Burns

written with Hal Goldman

G. P. Putnam's Sons
New York

G. P. Putnam's Sons
Publishers Since 1838
200 Madison Avenue
New York, NY 10016

"Old Bones" by John Hadley copyright © 1976 Tree
Publishing Co., Inc. All rights administered by Sony Music
Publishing, 8 Music Sq. W., Nashville, TN 37203.
Reprinted by permission of the publisher.

Library of Congress Cataloging-in-Publication Data

Burns, George, date.
Wisdom of the 90s / by George Burns written with
Hal Goldman.
p.   cm.
ISBN 0-399-13695-9 (alk. paper)
1. Burns, George, date.   2. Entertainers—Anecdotes.
3. Comedians—United States—Biography.
I. Goldman, Hal.
II. Title
PN2287.B87A3   1991a
792.7'028'092—dc20   91-18730 CIP
[B]

Printed in the United States of America
1   2   3   4   5   6   7   8   9   10

This book is printed on acid-free paper.
∞

This book is dedicated to all my schoolteachers. I learned something from each one of those four nice ladies.

Contents

◁～ೂ～▷

CONTENTS

Foreword

WELL, HERE I AM starting another book. If I had just said, "Here I am," it would have got your attention, and maybe even a round of applause. But the fact is I am starting another book. Everyone I've told this to has been very excited . . . all except my doctor. He frowned. I said, "Don't you like the idea of me starting a book?" He said, "Yes, but I'd like it better if you were starting an article." That was kind of disturbing. Why should I have a doctor who has so little confidence in himself?

Anyway, this will be my ninth book. And I'd like it to be a little different from the others. That's the creative side of me coming out. It's not that they haven't all sold well. I would have said it's not that they haven't all sold like hotcakes, but with everyone so worried about their cholesterol, who knows how hotcakes are selling these days?

So how can this book be different? And don't say, "Make it funny." My publisher, Phyllis Grann, already made that suggestion. She also came up with the title—"Wisdom of the 90s." I was for calling it "Still Alive at 95." I figured I could do a whole series of these. Next year it could be "Lots to Fix at 96." The year after—"Hello Heaven, I'm 97," followed by "98 and Doing Great!" Then, "Feeling Fine for 99."

When I'm 100 I won't have time to write a book. I'll be too busy playing that date I'm booked for at the London Palladium Theatre.

After much thought, staff consultation, and testing, Putnam's informed me they were sticking with "Wisdom of the 90s." It's a good title, but I am a little uncomfortable with it. Maybe that's because I never went past the fourth grade, still spell cat with two *t*'s, and have been called lots of things, but "wise" was never one of them. On the other hand, I've been around awhile, I've lived through a lot of history, I've known failure, I've known success, so I guess they figure that as I sit here at my desk thinking back over it all, I'm bound to have some observations that may be of interest to you.

Look, who am I to question my publisher? Selling books is their business, it's not mine. I've never made it a practice to stick my nose into things I know nothing about. Lots of performers these days are very active in politics. Not me. I stay out of it. Like I once said to President Coolidge, "I don't tell you how to run the country, and you don't tell me how to sing 'Red Rose Rag.'" He didn't crack a smile. That didn't bother me. Calvin was known for his lack of humor. What bothered me was when I got the same reaction from President Kennedy. What can you do, you win a few, you lose a lot.

While they were worrying about the title, I finally thought of a great way to make this book different—no chapters. Every book I've written so far has had chapters. I'm fed up with chapters. First of all, you have to think of a title for each chapter. I said that wrong. Since this is my book you don't have to think of a title for each chapter, I have to think of it. And being somewhat of a humorist, I'm expected to think of a *funny* title for each chapter. It's not easy thinking of funny chapter titles. In fact, it's a lot of extra work. And when you get to be my age the idea is to get the job done with as little work as possible. (Hey, that's a piece of wisdom! Maybe they're right about the title.)

There's something else that bothers me about chapters. They require too much planning. Before you put a word on paper, you have to lay out the whole book in your mind—decide what subject this chapter will cover and what subject that chapter will cover. How do I know ahead of time what I'll get out of a subject? What if I think I'll have enough on a subject to fill a chapter, and it turns out that I don't? Then I have to either drop the subject or try to squeeze it into a chapter where it may not belong. I've discovered that planning is fine when you're building a house, but when you're writing a book it can be a pain in the ass. (Oh-oh, another bit of wisdom. I'm blowing all my wisdom and I haven't even got to the book yet.)

Well, now you know what to expect. No chapters. No organized subjects. Just me rambling along wherever this ninety-five-year-old mind takes me. To break it up, after every ten pages or so I'll stop, and before I start up again there'll be a few pages with other things for you to look at. Picture this as a TV show of mine— I'm doing one of my monologues, only longer, and the pages in between are the commercials. Clever, isn't it. Excuse me, my phone is ringing.

That was Phyllis. I told her my plan, and she said, "George, what are you talking about? Neither of your last two books had chapter titles, and your last one was constructed like a long monologue!"

I've got to start reading my books. Well, it proves there's nothing new under the sun. It also proves my plan works, so when you turn the page, the monologue starts. . . .

Okay, so after the picture the monologue starts. Sue me, I have very good lawyers.

SEQUENCE I

Alan Berliner

When you're an author the writing never stops.

I PROBABLY SHOULDN'T BE starting my book with a statement that you may not believe, but I have to say it anyway. This year I'm ninety-five, and it doesn't bother me. I'm not happy about it. I'm not sad about it. I'm not proud of it. I'm not ashamed of it. It's just not something I'm preoccupied with. My entrances and exits . . . yes. My punch lines . . . yes. But not my age.

But then, I've never been one to dwell on my age. When another birthday comes along I make a wish, try to blow out the candles, and that's the end of it. I don't worry that I'm a year older. I rarely even think about it. There have been times in my life when I've actually forgotten my age. But all of a sudden I'm constantly being reminded of it. Everyone asks me how I feel now that I'm ninety-five.

I tell them I feel just as good at ninety-five as I felt when I was ninety-four. I like that answer. In fact, I like it so much that I sometimes give it without waiting for anyone to ask the question. Yesterday at my club I was barely in the door when a member greeted me with, "Hi, George, how does it feel to be ninety-five?"

I said, "I feel just as good as I felt when I was ninety-four."

Instead of laughing, he said, "Does that mean you feel good or you feel bad?" I said, "It's none of your business."

A minute later another member stopped me. "Good to see you, George. How does it feel to be ninety-five?" I said, "Herb, you're ninety-six—why are you asking me?" He said, "I forgot."

At least he remembered my name. And I remembered his. That's unusual for me. I have a tough time remembering names. But I'm not as bad at it as what's his name? . . . that fellow I was just talking about . . . what was it? . . . a short word . . . four letters . . . started with a P . . . no it was an H . . . Henry? . . . no that's five letters . . . an H . . . an H . . . four letters . . . what's that stuff they put on food to make it taste better? . . . Herbs! . . . that's it! Herb! I'm not as bad at remembering names as Herb.

I go through that a lot these days. And this problem with names is not a new one for me. In fact, it dates back to my grade-school teachers. I didn't have many during that brief scholastic career, but I still had trouble getting their names right—all except Miss Hollander, my third-grade teacher. I always knew her name. That must have been because I was in her class for so many years.

For some reason I wasn't too aware of my problem until ten or maybe fifteen years ago. Then I began noticing that what had been an occasional slipup on a name was becoming more frequent. And it was happening with people whose names it was more and more embarrassing for me to forget. Sometimes I'd remember the name, sometimes I wouldn't. So one day I said to myself, "Bill—no, no, you're George—George, why keep taking chances with the names, worrying that you'll forget them or get them wrong? From now on why not play it safe and call everyone 'Kid.'"

I thought that was a great idea, and that's what I've been doing ever since. I call everybody "Kid"—strangers, friends, young people, old people. . . . One day I ran into Adolph Zukor at the club. I shouted in his ear, "Good to see you, Kid!" He was 103 at the time.

It works out great. Nobody expects me to call them by their name anymore. They all know it's going to be "Kid." And when I call them that, they don't know that the odds are ten to one I've forgotten their name. They're happy, and I'm spared lots of embarrassment.

If I didn't have that going for me these days, I'd be embarrassed every two minutes. Now I'm *really* forgetting names, and of people who might be a little put out if they knew it—like performers I've known for ages, nextdoor neighbors, dinner companions, sleeping companions, my live-in couple, my secretary–office manager, who has been with me for thirty-two years. That's wrong, the Kid has been with me thirty-five years.

Unfortunately, there are some situations where the "Kid" saver doesn't apply. Say, for example, I'm at a cocktail party with two people I know. They're obviously waiting for me to introduce them to each other, and I can't do it because I've drawn a complete blank on one or both of their names. I've found myself in this embarrassing position so many times that I finally figured out what to do—stay away from cock-tail parties.

It happened to me just last week, and I wasn't at a party. I was in a restaurant having dinner with my son, Ronnie, when this old, old friend of mine from New York came over to my table. He was so happy to see me. But then it got awkward. I could see he was waiting for me to introduce him to Ronnie, but I just could not remember his name. I was never so embar-rassed. Who forgets his son's name?

Show me an elderly person and I'll show you some-one who can do forty minutes for you on his or her latest memory lapses. And if you're still around forty minutes later, you'll probably get to hear the whole thing all over again.

Old-age forgetfulness is the subject of jokes that must run into the thousands. Hardly a day goes by that I don't hear one or two of these knee-slappers. Like that one Barry Mirkin told me the other day. No, that was nothing—the one Jan Murray had, that was the funny one. I remember laughing when he told it to me. Now how did that go? . . . oh, yeah. These two old guys are sitting on a bench, and one of them . . . what am I doing, that was Barry's, it went no place. . . . Wait, it's coming to me . . . yeah, now I've got it! . . .

This is how it goes: It's ten in the morning, Sarah's in bed, and she says to her husband, "Sam, be a good boy, go to the deli and bring me a hot pastrami on rye."

"Hot pastrami on rye," he repeats.

"With lots of mustard," she says, "and write it down, you shouldn't forget."

Eldo

With my son, What's-his-name, in 1957. And here we are thirty-four years later. I *think* that's us in both pictures.

"I won't forget. You want a hot pastrami on rye with lots of mustard."

"And have them throw in a big kosher pickle."

"Fine," he says, and starts to walk out. She says, "Sam, you'll forget, write it down!" He says, "I don't have to write it down. You want a hot pastrami on rye with lots of mustard and a big kosher pickle." And out he goes. Twenty minutes later he's back with a plate of salami and eggs.

"Sam," she hollers, "I told you to write it down!"

"Why, what's wrong?"

She says, "You forgot the bagel!"

Some young people are reluctant to tell jokes like that. They're afraid it might be taken as a lack of concern for the wear and tear that old people have to put up with. From what I've seen, they couldn't be more wrong. Old people can't wait to tell these same jokes to each other. I don't know of any group less sensitive about themselves than the elderly, or more able to laugh at their shortcomings.

They say about athletes that the first thing to go is the legs. I find that with the aged the last thing to go is their sense of humor. Much of the material that I do in my stage show has to do with my age. I don't stop poking fun at myself. And my best audiences are in places like Sun City and Leisure World. They love it when I say things like, "If I'm making a movie, and the director wants me to cry, I think about my sex life. And if he wants me to laugh, I think about my sex life."

They understand that kind of humor. If they could, they'd be up there on the stage saying the same kind of things. Look, I can speak for the elderly. If I'm not one of them, who is? And I share their attitude. It's better to laugh at the wear and tear than it is to cry about it. You learn to roll with the punches. You have to.

Art Linkletter recently wrote a book, and he had a wonderful title—*Old Age Is Not for Sissies.* For some it is more of a curse than a blessing. For the lucky ones, like myself, there is still the wear and tear. This past year I've had my share—a dental bridge that took months of looking up at three different dentists to save—an ear that had to get used to living with a hearing aid—an eye that wasn't doing its job until I had the cataract removed.

Everything else still seems to be working. If I knew of something that wasn't, I'd tell you about it. I have very little to hide. I could have said that what I have left is so little I don't have to hide it. Everyone tells me I'm in great shape. I'll take their word for it. I have to—most of the time I'm too tired to argue with them.

Actually, I'm happy to say that I have no major health complaints. And I hope I haven't given you the wrong impression about my memory. It's not that bad. In fact, right now it is probably typical of others my age . . . that is, if there are others my age.

I do notice that aside from names, what is getting more difficult for me to recall are things that happened recently, like two minutes ago, a few hours ago, a few days ago. And yet something from fifty years ago I can remember as if it happened yesterday. Well, not yesterday, because that I can't remember. But what's to remember from yesterday? Whatever I did yester-

A group of my younger fans. They dig my jive.

day, what I did fifty years ago was more exciting, that I can guarantee.

Sometimes I'm amazed at the things that come back to me from my childhood. Like the time I hid under the bed when Miss Hollander came over to ask my mother why I hadn't been to school for two weeks. I knew why, I was singing with the PeeWee Quartet, and I didn't have time for school.

My mother didn't even know I was playing hooky, and she wasn't happy to get the news. After a minute I heard the front door open and then close. Mother hollered to me under the bed, "You can come out now, Miss Hollander's gone." So I came out, and there was Miss Hollander. What could I do? I sang her a song. Well, I would have, but my mother was too upset. She said she'd never trust me again. She'd never trust *me?!*

What would you say if I told you I find myself singing songs I haven't sung since my vaudeville days. Let's see . . . yeah, here's one. "Monkey Rag." Know when I last sang "Monkey Rag"? In 1915 at the Myrtle Theater in Brooklyn. I'm going to sing it for you. Here's the verse—fast, like I did it then:

Way down in Africa . . . Every evening in the bamboo trees . . . Some chimpanzees, monkey banjoes . . . Nightly they'd be strumming . . . They would be a humming . . . It was worse than buzzing bees . . . A big baboon had a band . . . It was the best in monkeyland . . . Played ragtime grand . . . This big baboon was requested to compose a tune . . . One night in June . . . And so he wrote a tune that's honky

. . . He called the thing the monkey . . . And gave it to his band to play . . . Oh oh that night was a sight . . . All the monkeys began to swing and sway. . . .

There you are. Haven't sung that in seventy-six years and I didn't miss a word. If you don't believe me, here's the stamp of the notary who witnessed it.

I should tell you something else. I was never able to read too well. And that's not because I left school in the fourth grade, it's because I'm dyslectic. Not too long ago I would have stopped there and said, "And you thought I was Jewish." But I've reached the stage where I feel that I don't have to be funny every minute. Every two minutes is enough. Anyway, I am dyslectic. (I'm also Jewish for those of you who didn't know. And for those of you who did know, too. That takes care of the next four minutes.)

They didn't know about dyslexia when I was a child. Now they can help kids overcome this condition, which causes your eye to transpose the letters and words you are trying to read. On my own some-how I've managed to work it out to some extent, but reading always was, and still is, a slow process for me.

We all know about blind people compensating for their lack of sight by learning to hear better than those with normal vision. Because reading was hard for me, I concentrated on improving my memory. As time went on, it got better and better, and I found I could depend on it more and more. Learning my vaudeville sketches and monologues was no problem for me. And when Gracie and I went into radio, I would hold my script like everyone else around the microphone, but that was just for looks — I had memo-rized all my lines. Then when television came along, while the radio actors who were used to just reading their scripts now had trouble learning all their lines, it was a breeze for me. Then again, with Gracie around I didn't have too many lines to learn. With my movies there were pages and pages to memorize every day, but that was no problem for me, either. Nowadays it would take more effort, but here again compensation enters in. If I'm getting paid, I remember.

Well, what do you say we take a break? I think I'll go to my club for lunch. I'd invite you to come with me, but after digesting everything I've said so far, you're probably not hungry. See you tomorrow.

INTERLUDE

The Ten Wisest Men
of All Time

1. King Solomon

Any man who could keep 1,000 wives happy without any of them suspecting what he was up to deserves to be at the top of the list.

2. Napoleon

He was the master of deception. By always holding his hand under his jacket, he fooled everyone into thinking that was where he kept his wallet, when all the time it was in his pants pocket.

3. Ray Kroc

He founded the worldwide McDonald's restaurants. In 1955 he sold his first hamburger, and by 1991 the count was 80,000,000,000 of them. Incidentally, the inclusion of Mr. Kroc in this list was not endorsed by the UOAC (Union of American Cows).

4. Peter Minuit

A genius in real estate. He talked Chief Running Water into selling the island of Manhattan for $24 in trinkets. The chief wanted him to throw in a naked picture of Mrs. Minuit, but Peter held out.

5. Johnny Carson

The less Johnny worked, the more NBC wanted him. He went from five days a week to four, and then to three. But he quit too soon. They were going to give him another raise not to come in at all.

6. Thomas Alva Edison

Brilliant inventor. His favorite creation was the phonograph. He only invented the light bulb so he could see where to place the needle on the records.

7. Mahatma Gandhi

He thought up and organized India's nonviolent resistance movement. But the smartest thing Mahatma did was wearing that sheet all the time. Saved a fortune in laundry bills.

8. Don Rickles

He must be smart. He's insulted everyone around and he still has his original teeth.

9. The Sponsor of the Burns and Allen Radio Show

10. The Sponsor of the Burns and Allen TV Show

Alan Berlit

The Eleventh-Wisest Man of All Time. He's too modest to turn around and let us see who he is.

The Wisest Women
of All Time

The Wives of King Solomon

They knew what he was up to all the time.

The Dumbest Man
of All Time

Chief Running Water

He blew it. He could have got that picture, too.

SEQUENCE II

IT'S ME AGAIN. I'm kind of tired this morning. I rarely go to parties, but last night I went to a big one, and I didn't get home until ten o'clock.

When I don't go out I'm usually in bed by nine. That's not because of my age. Going to bed early is somethi-g I've gotten used to. I've been doing it for years. I'm not the only one. Everyone thinks that here in Hollywood we lead these wild lives, staying up all hours of the night. Not true. I have actor friends who are seldom in bed before midnight, but I know others, younger than myself, who can't wait to get to bed. Warren Beatty told me that some nights it might be a little later, but there are lots of nights he's in bed by eight o'clock. I guess it depends who he's in bed with.

The party I went to last night was at the home of a couple who are very nice, and very, very wealthy. Their house is like a hotel, and if the grounds were any larger, by now the Japanese would have bought it for a golf course. Off the patio there's an eighty-foot pool. And that's the Jacuzzi.

They're in the papers all the time for their lavish parties. I knew this going to be one of their smaller ones when I got the invitation three months ago. It was cute, but I doubt that it cost over seventy-five dollars. I must be on their B-list. But I felt I had to go. This was the fourth invitation they've sent me this year, and how many times can you say you'll be out of town doing a show?

As I suspected, it was not one of their typical lavish parties. There were only two orchestras playing — the circus they brought in to keep things going during the intermissions didn't have any elephants — and while they usually put out enough food to feed an army, this time there was barely enough for a battalion.

How many guests did they have? I'd say there had to be five hundred, and I'm pretty good at counting a house. As you can imagine, the place was loaded with celebrities. I knew lots of them. I even introduced five or six to the hosts.

Standing around for any length of time hurts my back, so during the cocktail hour at parties like this one I grab a martini and find a chair for myself. If I've come with someone, they sit with me. If not, I don't mind because people are always coming over to talk to me. People I know, but also total strangers.

So last night this cute young thing bounces up to me, and she goes (these kids don't say, they go) — she goes, "Wow! George Burns! I just had to come over and steal a kiss!" She plants one on my cheek, and then she goes, "Wow! What a thrill! George, you are really amazing! I mean like . . . how do you do it?!"

How do you do it? That's a question that can be taken two ways. And when I'm asked how I do it by a pretty young girl I like to have a little fun with my answer. So I said, "What makes you think I still do it? Maybe it's years since I've done it. Maybe it's been so long that I can't remember what I was doing when I did it." I was just getting rolling when a good-looking young fellow came by and took her away. I didn't have a chance to ask if he was her husband. If she had said he was, I could have said, "Good, then you can cheat on him."

I get away with talk like that. Girls love it. And do you know why? Because at my age I'm harmless. They know I have to be kidding around. If that good-looking young fellow said the same things to a woman, he'd get his face slapped. With me it's said in fun, and taken in fun.

Being able to do risqué humor is one of the advantages of being old. It rates up there with Medicare, Senior Citizen Discounts and Early Bird Dinners.

Look at "The Golden Girls." That's one of the funniest shows on the air, and also the dirtiest. Bea Arthur, Rue McClanahan, Betty White, and Estelle Getty have lines that no other actresses would be allowed to say. They talk about orgasms, erections, hemorrhoids, body odor, their periods — anything and everything. They get away with it because the characters they play are likable old ladies, and the one who gets away with the most is the oldest, Bea Arthur's mother.

I should be able to get away with even more than Bea Arthur's mother, because I'm older than Bea Arthur's mother. I probably could, but I don't try. My stuff is less direct. I come at it in a different way. I don't say it dirty, I let the audience make it dirty. If I'm on stage trying to raise my microphone, and I say, "I got it down, but I can't get it up," I haven't said anything dirty. I'm talking about the microphone. If the audience wants to take it dirty, that's their business. I may help them a little by taking an extra-long puff on my cigar.

What you can get away with depends on who you are and how you come across to people. Remember Mae West? One of the biggest laughs she ever got in a theater was when she said, "When I'm good I'm good. When I'm bad I'm better." Coming from her, with that overblown figure, that nonstop wiggle, and that breathy way of talking, it was a perfect line. You knew she wasn't playing it for real.

If Lauren Bacall did that line, it would lose the fun, but at least it would be believable. She's letting you know that she can do a pretty good job under the covers. Coming from Grace Kelly the same line would have been totally jarring. Too pretty, too sweet. You'd resent them for making her say it.

Then there was the case of Fred Allen. No one could do lines as witty as Fred, and they were all based on sarcasm and cutting putdowns. During his famous radio feud with Jack Benny, they were arguing about who was funnier, and when Fred said, "Benny, you couldn't ad-lib a belch after a Hungarian dinner," the listeners howled. Fred loved taking network vice-presidents apart. He'd say, "A network vice-president comes into his office in the morning, finds a molehill on his desk, and by nightfall he's made a mountain out of it."

As long as the people were hearing Fred make all those cracks over their radios, they thought he was hilarious. But for TV he had a problem. Although there was never a nicer person than Fred Allen, he happened to have a sour, mean-looking face. So on television, when the viewers saw him saying all those sarcastic things, instead of coming off funny, he came off as an unlikable crank. What worked in radio didn't work for the same person on television.

In show business you have to know what you can and can't get away with. Those old motion-picture superstars all knew that. They knew exactly what kind of roles the public would accept them in. So did their studios. And if they didn't, I would have been glad to tell them what their stars could play. I can just see myself doing that for MGM or Fox, or Warner Bros. I could have really helped them:

"You say you can't find anyone that's right for the main character . . . the fast-talking tobacco auctioneer? No problem—Jimmy Stewart. I can just see him doing it.

"What's next? You need a timid bookkeeper with thick glasses? I've got your man—John Wayne. He could also play that cowardly little Mexican bandit in the other picture. Then again, Gary Cooper might be better for that one.

"What else? You're looking for someone to be a tough, foul-mouthed hooker? Stop looking, Irene Dunne's perfect for that. If she's busy, call Helen Hayes.

"What's that? You got a salt-of-the-earth Irish priest and his boyhood pal who becomes a cocky gangster? That's a cinch—Jimmy Cagney for the priest and Pat O'Brien for the gangster."

I missed the boat. I should have been a casting director. But who knows if any studio would have hired me as a casting director. They never even gave me a part where I played one.

Why did I go through all that? Now I've lost the point I was going to make. At least I'm not playing bridge. When I lose a point there it costs me three cents. Wait . . . now I remember what I was getting to—that what you can get away with doesn't just apply to show business, or any business. It also applies to everyone in their everyday lives.

I'm sure most of you women know someone, let's say a lady acquaintance of yours, who prides herself on telling it like it is. When you bump into her she'll always hit you with something like, "I almost didn't recognize you, you've gained so much weight." . . . or, "You better see a doctor, I hate those black circles under your eyes." . . . or, "You know, your friend Amy has that same skirt, but she has the legs for it." She's always blurting out things like that, and you hate her for it. You cross the street when you see her coming.

But then you have another lady friend who you admire for telling you the same kind of things. You think, "That's a real friend. She cares enough to come right out and say what's best for me." Maybe it's a difference in the way they say it, or in their person-alities, or in your past experiences with them—whatever the reason, one gets away with it and one doesn't.

You have to know who you are. And whoever you are, it's better to make the best of it than to try to be somebody you're not.

Until I was twenty-seven I didn't know who I was. Neither did anyone else. In those days I wasn't doing well, and to get work I had to keep changing my name. I changed my name so often that I never got any mail. Nobody knew who to write to.

I was Joe Brown of Brown and Williams, Singers, Dancers and Rollerskaters. I was Harry Pierce in a singing act. I did a seal act, Captain Blue and Flipper — I was Captain Blue. When the act didn't catch on I made a change. I became Captain Betts. It didn't help. I was Barney Darnell . . . Maxey Kline . . . Willy Bogart. It got so I wasn't only stealing jokes, I was stealing names.

All that changed when the act became George Burns and Gracie Allen. From that day on I've known who I am. Learning *what* I am took a little longer, but I finally figured that out, too. I now know what I am, and I know that if I try to be anything else, it doesn't work. And that goes for off stage as well as on.

I can't be anything but what I am; someone who smokes his cigars, takes it easy, doesn't sweat, doesn't jump around and make funny faces, someone who kids himself instead of trying to get laughs at the expense of others, and most of all, someone who knows his age, acts his age, and accepts his age.

I have to tell you that being old isn't such a handicap. In some ways it's a help. You can't do as much, and there may be things you can't do as well, but nobody expects you to. Old-timers don't have to come in first. They get credit for just showing up. And if they're out there making a real effort, they've got everyone pulling for them.

I can honestly say that never in my entire career have I felt the public affection and support that I feel these days. When I walk out on the stage to do my show I get a standing ovation before I open my mouth. Why are they applauding? Because I made it to the center of the stage? It could be. Some nights it's not that easy. Then again, maybe they're applauding because they don't see too many ninety-five-year-olds who are willing and able to come out and face a live audience.

The standing ovation I get at the end of my show is something else. That's because I pulled it off. For an hour I made them laugh and entertained them. That's the ovation I appreciate the most. But that first one isn't bad, either.

Well, I'm off to my club again. When I enter the dining room they better give me a standing ovation. If they don't, I'll stop paying my dues.

INTERLUDE

Nuggets of Wisdom[*]

Bridge is a game that separates the men from the boys. It also separates husbands and wives.

—G. Burns

Happiness is having a legitimate excuse for not attending a Bar Mitzvah.

—G. Burns

[*]I realize these are often referred to as pearls. I prefer to refer to mine as nuggets. If I say I have a pearl of wisdom, it better be sensational. With a nugget I'm not sticking my neck out so far.

Grooming Tips for the Over-90 Set

Dress simply. If you wear a dinner jacket, don't wear anything else on it . . . like lunch or dinner.

There are exceptions to the rule of simplicity. It would not be wrong to wear a lapel button that says, "Help me find my glasses."

Neatness is all-important. Keep your mustache short and well trimmed. This bit of advice also applies to men.

Low-cut dresses are definitely out. This applies to men, too.

Avoid moth holes. A bad fall could do you in.

Be cautious about the clothes you buy. A T-shirt that says, "Help me use it so I don't lose it," is worse than inappropriate, and it's a waste of money.

Take care not to wear stripes that are out of sync with your wrinkles.

When in doubt, carry an umbrella. The added weight of wet clothes can make the knees buckle.

To avoid dandruff falling on your shoulders, step nimbly to one side.

To prevent bags in the knees, walk backwards.

For formal affairs it is still proper to wear a cummerbund around your waist. However, using it for a truss would be frowned upon.

SEQUENCE III

Long Photography

I got this the same year I had my triple bypass. I think I liked this better.

ARE YOU STILL with me? Good, because I wanted to talk to you about something I've never been able to understand—why it is that so many people spend their days living in the past. Not just older people, either. And their past may not have been that great. It doesn't matter. They are constantly looking back. You see them, grown-up men who sit at their desks replaying that punt they returned in the big Homecoming game; middle-aged mothers who can't get past their big moment in that high-school play.

I have a neighbor who went on a cruise with his wife years ago, and can't forget that he came in second in the big Ping-Pong tournament. I'll admit that's quite an accomplishment, but how many times do I have to hear about it? And with every detail—the slippery deck, the waves, how he came from 6 points behind and got even at 20 to 20, how the wind caught his next serve and the ball went overboard (it should have happened to him), and how he finally pulled the match out to wild applause from the other four contestants. That's all he talks about. Pardon me, the last time I saw him he did mention one other thing. He told me that he and his wife have very few friends.

I don't believe in looking back. I look ahead to what I'm going to do tomorrow, next week, next month.

That gets my adrenaline going. And these days getting my adrenaline going is a little harder than getting my car started.

I won't say that I never look back. When a great-looking girl walks past me on the street, I look back. I looked back at one the other day in Beverly Hills, walked into a post, banged up my nose, and broke my glasses. That won't happen again. The next time I look back I'll stop walking. The new pair of glasses I had to buy cost me $83. But it was worth it. What a body!

I don't want to be a crank about this. If you don't overdo it, there's nothing wrong with looking back. There are lots of things from the past that come to my mind, wonderful memories that . . . that will have to wait because I have to go to the bathroom. Hal, you take over for me. . . . Yes, I mean it. Go ahead, the show must go on. . . .

Hi—I'm Hal. I wasn't expecting this. I knew I'd be helping George when he wrote this book, but I didn't think I'd be helping him when he went to the bathroom. I don't mean that the way it sounded. I wouldn't help George go to the bathroom. He doesn't need anyone to help him go to the bathroom. When the day comes that he does, and it may be sooner than later, I'll help him go to the bathroom.

I'll have to, it's in my contract. Even if it weren't in my contract, I'd do it. I'd do anything for George Burns, even lie, which I just did. I don't have a contract with George Burns. His

Alan Berliner

Notice I'm not looking back. On the next page, you'll see why.

Alan Berliner

lawyers told him that the one he wanted them to draw up would be thrown out of court. And he wouldn't go for the one I wanted to draw up. So I've been working for him twelve years on a handshake. It's a very loose arrangement. He only insists on one thing: that I get to the office before he does so I can give him a standing ovation when he comes in.

This is great. Now I can tell you a few things about that sweet old man and he'll never know. Twelve years I've been with him, and do you know what he got me for Christmas? A deck of ———— oh-oh, here he comes. Go ahead, George, you're on. . . .

Okay, everyone, I'm back. Where was I? Hal, I know I was in the bathroom! I meant what was I talking about? A few more remarks like that and I'm taking him off my Christmas list.

Let's see . . . oh yeah, now I remember. I was saying I have some wonderful memories. The night Gracie decided to marry me. Our wedding day. And that first time Gracie and I played the Palace.

This was it! The Big Time! Jack Benny, Mary Kelly, Rena Arnold, Cary Grant (who was still Archie Leach), Blossom Seeley, and Benny Fields were all there for opening night. We saw to that. In vaudeville the bigger the act, the later it came on. We were third on the bill, but who cared? To get on the Palace bill at all, they must have thought you were pretty good. I must have thought so too. When Benny and Blossom asked when they should send their flowers up to Gracie, I said, "After our second encore." That line could have come out of Al Jolson's mouth. But he was across the street at the Wintergarden saying, "Ladies and gentlemen—you ain't heard nothing yet!"

There are things I recall that make my chest swell so much that I could wear Arnold Schwarzenegger's shirts. The night I got up to accept the Oscar for Best Supporting Actor in *The Sunshine Boys*. I was eighty years old then, and they gave me a tremendous hand. I kept it brief, but I remember saying, "Getting this award tonight proves one thing: if you stay in this business long enough, and if you can get to be old enough, you get to be new again." Big laugh. I also said, "The last picture I made for MGM was thirty-seven years ago, and making *The Sunshine Boys* was so exciting that I've decided from now on I'm going to make a picture every thirty-seven years." Another big laugh. Walking off that stage I was pretty happy with myself. Not for winning the Oscar, but for getting those two laughs.

There was another movie that comes back to me— *Going in Style*—the one I co-starred in with Art Carney and Lee Strasberg. The night before Lee and I were to play our first scene together, our young director, Martin Brest, came to me and said he had a problem and he didn't quite know how to handle it. When I asked him what the problem was, he told me that Lee was very nervous about having to do the scene with me. I said, "Martin, I know Lee Strasberg is a great actor and he's taught our finest actors in his school, but what's he so worried about? Does he think

Peter C. Borsari

Could Lee have been right? Maybe I *was* too good to work with him.

I'm that bad?" Martin said, "No, he's worried that you're too good."

That's a nice thing to remember, too. Hard to believe, but nice. But then there are things I remember that I'd just as soon forget. Like one time at the Jefferson Theater on 33rd Street in New York. I was working alone then, doing a dancing act. My name was Willie Delight. I don't know what happened, but I did my first show and my fly was open. That was embarrassing, but the most embarrassing thing was when I did my second show with my fly closed and the manager canceled me.

I remember a thing that happened when I was doing a singing-dancing act called Harry Jones and the Millishap Sisters. I did bad acts, but I picked out good names. I was having lunch one day at Wienig's Restaurant and a guy walked in and sold me a drop, a piece of scenery. In those days if you did a vaudeville act, no matter what your salary was, if you carried your own scenery, you got an extra $50 a week. So I bought this drop for $50. I couldn't get into a subway with it, and I didn't have money for a taxi. I had to walk with the drop on my back from Wienig's on 42nd Street to the theater on 14th Street. The stagehands were gone. I couldn't hang up the drop, so we rehearsed our music, and I didn't get to see the drop hanging up until the show. It was a church, and in the middle was a door, a cutaway entrance.

I told one Millishap sister to come in from stage left, the other from stage right, and I would come in through the center. I went to go through the center, and it was solid curtain. No cutaway. I couldn't get through, I had to run around and come out. It was not one of my greatest entrances. After the show I offered to sell the drop for $25, but nobody would buy it.

There are also some people I'd just as soon forget. Vaudeville had many great monologists. Of them all, Frank Fay would have to be considered the greatest. That's not just my opinion, it was his, too. He was also the most arrogant monologist in vaudeville. You can make that the most arrogant performer in vaudeville.

One time he was testifying in court, and when he was asked his occupation by the opposing lawyer, he said, "I'm the greatest comedian in the world." Later, his own lawyer asked him why he would make a statement like that, and he said, "What could I do? I was under oath." That tells you the size of his ego.

Besides being egotistical and arrogant, Frank had another endearing quality. He could be brutally sarcastic. And his sarcasm reflected his arrogance. When he put you down, it was as though he didn't even want to bother with someone so obviously beneath him.

Our paths first crossed one time when Gracie and I played the Palace. He had been the m.c. there for months, doing the kind of job only a Frank Fay could do. While we performed, he stood in the wings watching. After we finished the act, he sauntered over to us and, ignoring me, he took Gracie's hand and began telling her how impressed he was with everything about her—her unique delivery, her engaging personality, her delicate charm. He couldn't stop complimenting her. And then, still not giving me so much as a glance, he leaned toward her, and she leaned toward him, and he said, "But where did you get the man?"

There was only one Frank Fay. One was enough. There are some others I'd like to forget, but I forget who they are.

INTERLUDE

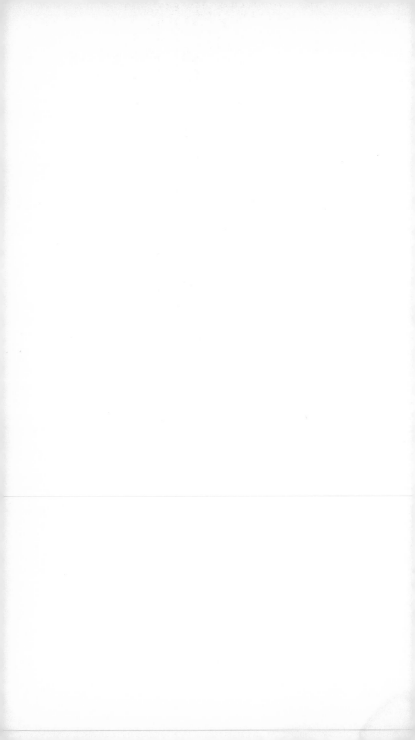

Nuggets of Wisdom

If what pleases some didn't make others miserable, you wouldn't have the world divided into Smoking and No Smoking.

—G. Burns

Everything that goes up must come down. But there comes a time when not everything that's down can come up.

—G. Burns

Ten Don'ts for a Long Life

DON'T SMOKE
DON'T DRINK
DON'T GAMBLE
DON'T EAT SALT
DON'T EAT SUGAR
DON'T EAT FATS
DON'T OVEREXERCISE
DON'T OVEREAT
DON'T UNDEREAT
DON'T PLAY AROUND

Author's Note

You may not live longer, but it will seem longer.

I have to show you what you shouldn't do, don't I?

Alan Berliner

Alan Berliner

—And you shouldn't do this, either.

Alan Berliner

—Or this.

SEQUENCE IV

Eldo

Conrad about to drive me to Hillcrest. I'm not even in the car and he's laughing.

WELL, WHAT'LL IT BE this time? I can talk about my career, I can talk about myself, or I can talk about two minutes.

That wasn't too funny, but it's only ten in the morning, and I don't get funny until around eleven-thirty. By noon I'm a riot. The trouble is, by then I'm on the way to my club, so the only one who gets to hear me is my driver. Yesterday he was laughing so hard he almost drove us under the back end of one of those heavy iron flatbed trucks. I said, "What the hell are you doing, Conrad?! If I want a convertible, I'll buy one!" That made him laugh some more and he backed into the car behind us. I said, "Conrad, for this I don't need you—I could drive myself." More laughter.

I'll have to get a new bumper, but fortunately there was no damage to the other car. The rest of the way to the club, while Conrad was laughing, I was thinking about letting him go, but how can you fire such a good audience? That was one of the reasons I hired him.

The truth is he's a good kid, and I do need him or some other driver because I don't drive anymore. Two years ago, when I had four accidents in one month, something told me that it was time to give it up. Actually, only three of those accidents were my fault.

The fourth was the fault of a feeble man who kept assuring me that it wouldn't have happened if he hadn't blacked out.

Don't ask me why I insisted on driving a car at the age of ninety-three. No, go ahead and ask me. And while you're at it, ask the Department of Motor Vehicles why they allowed me to drive a car at the age of ninety-three.

I shouldn't have been allowed to drive a car when I was forty-three—or thirty-three. I was a terrible driver. I not only went too fast, but my mind was always on shows and scripts, so I was constantly making left turns when I was signaling right turns. But at least in those days I could see over the steering wheel. By ninety-three it was ridiculous. My car was known as the Phantom Cadillac. People would see it whizzing by and they'd swear there was no driver.

Look, who am I kidding? I kept driving because I couldn't admit to myself that I'd become too old to do it. It's a thing called male pride. There are lots of old codgers around who have it, and lots more who aren't around because they had it. You see them every day—not the ones that aren't still around, the others—they're out on that dance floor flinging their partners around, on the tennis court and the jogging paths, pounding away. Their tongues are hanging out, but they're going to prove that they are still as good as ever.

That's one extreme. The other is just as bad, and probably more common. I'm talking about the senior citizens who think that because they are up in years they are not supposed to get out of their rocking chairs. Things they've done all their lives they stop doing. Everything is suddenly too much for them. They're afraid to move, afraid to go anywhere. They are alive, but they're not living.

I don't believe in that. I may have to cut down, but I don't stop. I still walk around my pool every day, but instead of going around it twenty times like I used to, I now go around it ten times. I still do my exercises every morning, but instead of thirty minutes, I've cut that to fifteen minutes. It's the same with sex. I only talk about it half as much as I did five years ago.

As I already told you, I have stopped driving. But that's balanced off by a whole new activity that I've taken up lately—going to doctors. Not that I've never gone to doctors before. I went to a doctor once about some difficulty I was having clearing my throat. When he told me to quit smoking I went to another doctor for a second opinion. This time I was a little more careful. I didn't just pick any doctor, I made sure I went to one who smoked. When I told that one about my throat problem he told me to forget it. I did, and it went away.

Then about seventeen years ago I was attended to by a whole team of doctors. That was when I had to have a triple heart bypass. Fortunately, my team won.

So I have been to doctors, but never like the past year or so. Some weeks I see doctors four or five days in a row, sometimes twice a day. I build my whole schedule around doctor appointments. It's become a way of life. And it's quite exciting. I get to learn all about diseases I'd never heard of, I meet lots of interesting people in waiting rooms, and I have my pulse felt by lots of pretty nurses. It's getting so if I have a day without a doctor's appointment, I feel let down.

Except for spending so much time in doctors' offices, my daily routine is much the same as it has been for the last twenty-five years. Before that it was a whole different thing. Then I was not only doing my role every week in the Burns and Allen show, but I was also wearing a producer's hat and a writer's hat. I would have worn a director's hat, too, but his hat didn't fit me. That's supposed to be a joke.

But the fact is I did co-produce and help write five weekly situation comedies—"The Bob Cummings Show," "Mister Ed," starring Alan Young, "Wendy and Me," starring Connie Stevens, "The People's Choice," starring Jackie Cooper, and "Mona McLuskey," starring Juliet Prowse. Sometimes I was so busy I didn't know what day it was. Now when I don't know what day it is, it's for a different reason.

When I took off all those hats, my life immediately calmed down, and as I said, it hasn't varied much since. Basically it's the same daily routine: Around six every morning I wake up. If you don't wake up, the rest of the routine is out the window. After doing my shortened exercises and taking my briefer walk around the pool, I play with the cats. That's a little less also, because one of my three cats has gone up to Pussy Paradise. Then comes breakfast. The cats eat more than I do. On a hungry morning I'll put away four prunes and a cup of coffee. After breakfast I thank Arlette—she's the cooking half of Daniel and Arlette, my live-in couple—and then Conrad comes by and drives me to the office. No laughing. I told you I don't

Sometimes you can overwork. This is how I looked when I wore all those hats.

Conrad

This is Willie. He's jealous of me because he only has nine lives.

get funny until around eleven-thirty. You have to remember these things.

I put in two hours at the office, from ten to twelve, the same as I've done for years. Hal usually sticks it out for the whole two hours, which I appreciate because he's not too funny until eleven-thirty, either. There's always something to keep us busy: a commercial to go over, a special to write, or one of these books that keep coming up. On top of that I have to make time for phone interviews and answering my fan mail.

After the office it's off to the club with Conrad at the wheel—but you already know about that. At the club, after telling various members how it feels to be ninety-five, I have lunch—maybe half a bagel and coffee, or a cup of soup and coffee. I have definitely cut down on lunch, partly because I'm less hungry these days, and partly because I can't wait to get to my bridge game.

Sometimes there are four of us, sometimes there are one or two more cutting in, but they are all the same members I've been playing with for years. I don't know their exact ages, but I don't have to tell them how it feels to be ninety-five. If I did, they wouldn't hear me. "Artie," I said to one of them yesterday, "you just dropped two cards." He said, "Thanks, George, and you look good, too." But I enjoy their company, and I enjoy the challenge of the game. It's the highlight of my day.

Bridge is the only game I play. I used to play golf, but I gave that up long ago. I tried. For years I tried. I wore the knickers, I had the big bag and all the clubs. But I was as pathetic with a three-wood as I was behind the wheel of my car.

A writing session with Hal. It's not always this hilarious.

Conrad

A hot game at Hillcrest. They just revised their no-smoking rule to permit it for all members over ninety-five. Great club.

Everyone at the club that I played with was pathetic—Jack Benny, Danny Kaye, the Ritz Brothers, Georgie Jessel. But they took it seriously. I didn't. They felt sorry for themselves. I only felt sorry for our pro, Eric Monti. He had to give us lessons.

I was on a green once with Jack Benny, and he missed his putt. When I say he missed it, I mean he didn't hit the ball. He almost cried. He should have. Whoever heard of whiffing a putt? And poor Jessel. He never could break 100. It was always 110 or 120. One day I was in the locker room, and he came running over to me all excited. "I did it, I did it!" he screamed. "I came in with a ninety-nine!" I said, "That's great, Georgie, how did you do it?" He said, "I'll tell you how I did it—every shot *perfect!*"

By three o'clock I'm home from the club and in bed for a two-hour nap. If I won at bridge, I fall right to sleep. If I lost, it takes a little longer. By a quarter to five I'm a new man. That's because I'm still dreaming. They don't wake me until five.

I get dressed, go downstairs and have a martini. That's a cut. I used to have two. I relax for an hour, watch the news, have my one big meal of the day, and I'm in bed by nine. That's if I don't go out. Once or twice a week I go out for dinner with a few good friends. Like tonight I'll be at Chasen's with Carol Channing and her husband, Charlie Lowe, Betty White and Barry Mirkin, Jerry Zeitman and his date. Other nights there might be just Barry and me and one other couple—Irving and Norma Brecher, or Walter and Carol Matthau, or Bob and Dolores Hope. I enjoy these evenings. I always have lots of laughs,

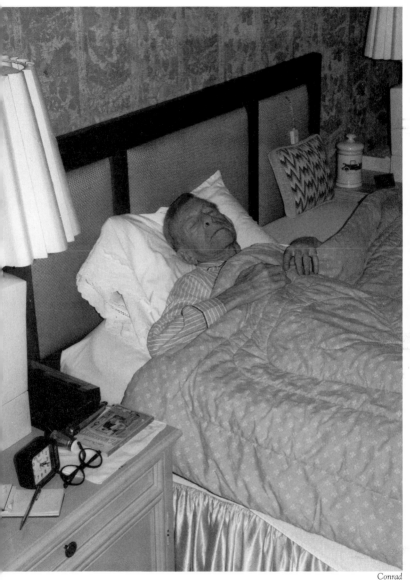

Conrad

Don't get nervous. It's just my daily nap.

At Chasen's. Thursday night out with Carol Channing (wearing the small hat), Barry Mirkin, and Charles Lowe.

sign lots of autographs, and sometimes I'm in such a good mood I even sign the dinner check.

I used to go out more—to benefits, roasts, parties given by fellow comedians. There's one going on every two minutes. I still go to a few, but that's what I've cut down on the most. I can't go to so many affairs, I barely have the energy to turn down the invitations.

Well, that's a typical day of mine. I've accounted for all but about twenty minutes of my time—that's for lighting all those cigars I still smoke.

And, of course, this schedule doesn't apply to the days I'm performing. And I'm happy to say that's still a lot of days. I did a TV special this year, I still do commercials, I appear on more talk shows than ever, and best of all, I still play a lot of dates doing my stage show. In fact, I just signed a two-year deal with the Riviera Hotel in Las Vegas. They wanted to make it five years, but I said, "What's the rush? If you gentlemen are still around two years from now, we'll talk about it."

On stage, after the opening act, usually a female singer, I'm out there alone for the rest of the show. That's a whole hour, and with my weak back, standing up that long eventually became a real problem. I was beginning to wonder how much longer I could still do it.

Then about two years ago, my manager, Irving Fein, suggested that after standing the first ten minutes or so, I should sit down for the rest of the show.

I told him he was crazy. I'm a stand-up comedian, not a sit-up comedian—my material wouldn't be effective sitting down. Well, he finally talked me into it.

And I have to admit, the laughs I get sitting down are the same laughs I got standing up. And the songs I do go over just as well. The only difference is sitting down I'm half as tired. And that means I'm going to keep on doing my show as long as there are enough customers out front to pay for the price of a chair.

And when the time comes that I can't do my show sitting down, you know what I'll do. I'll have them haul a bed out there, and I'll do it lying down.

Okay? Okay. Conrad, come on, see if you can get me to the club. Look, he's laughing already.

INTERLUDE

Wisdom Test

1. There are four cats on a fence. Three decide to jump. How many are left?

2. What does Mexico produce more than any other country?

3. Why does a stork stand on one foot?

4. What should a woman do to have beautiful hands?

5. Why do the swallows always return to San Juan Capistrano on March 19th?

6. Where was the Declaration of Independence signed?

7. What did Caesar say when Brutus stabbed him?

8. When is the "happy hour" at Dean Martin's house?

9. What was George Washington's farewell address?

10. Why is a rabbit's nose shiny?

11. For what was Louis the Fourteenth largely responsible?

12. What naughty thing did Adam and Eve do after they left the Garden of Eden?

13. What is a man who speaks seven dead languages called?

14. What kind of a nut loves to watch topless dancers?

1. Four. The three that decided to jump, didn't.

2. Mexicans.

3. Because if he lifted the other foot, he'd fall on his can.

4. Nothing.

5. To get their pictures in the paper on March 20th.

6. At the bottom.

7. "Ouch!"

8. From dawn to dusk and from dusk to dawn.

9. Heaven.

10. His powder puff is at the other end.

11. Louis the Fifteenth.

12. They raised Cain.

13. A very sociable corpse.

14. A chestnut.

Alan Berliner

Question: Which of these girls has a college degree?
Answer: Who cares?

Alan Berliner

Question: Are they too old for our author?
Answer: Yes, but he believes rules are made to be broken.

Question: These girls have spent a number of evenings with our author. What did Kitty Kelley find out he did with them? Answer: Played bridge.

SEQUENCE V

WHEN YOU'VE DONE something for a long time you're bound to know more about it than when you started. That's why when it comes to doctors I don't want the young ones, I want the ones who have been around awhile. Why they want me I have no idea.

What goes for the practice of medicine also goes for my line of work. I've only been in show business eighty-eight years, but I've already learned a few things about it.

One thing I've learned is the importance of openings and closings. Show business is like sex — you need a good start and a big finish. Hey, that's not a bad line. I should have used it instead of the one I opened with at the top of this page. Anytime you can work sex into an opening you've got it made. I'm not saying you can't have a good opening without sex. That's silly. If I said you can't have sex without a good opening, that would make more sense. But I wouldn't say that. I do a clean act.

In vaudeville there were lots of great openings and great finishes. I told about dozens of them in my last book, *All My Best Friends.* It's loaded with hilarious stuff about vaudeville and my years since then. If you haven't read it yet, buy a copy, you'll get a kick out of it. (I've also learned that a good plug never hurts.)

Gracie and I had a great opening for our vaudeville act. We came out holding hands, and as we got near stage center Gracie stopped, looked back, and waved at someone she saw standing in the wings. She left me and went toward a man who came out and met her at the side of the stage. He kissed her, and she kissed him. He left the stage, and she came back to me and said, "Who was that?" It not only got a tremendous laugh, but it set her whole character. With just three words the audience knew what to expect from Gracie Allen.

We also had a finish that never missed. You may have seen a version of it at the end of our Burns and Allen television show. I'd ask her something, usually about her family, and we'd get into a routine where she gave answers that made sense to her, but not to anyone else. Then when things got really confusing, which they always did, I'd give up and say, "Say goodnight, Gracie." And she'd say, "Goodnight, Gracie."

I've worked out a very good finish for the stage show I do these days. I'm not going to tell you what it is, because some of you may not have seen my show yet. That's another thing I've learned—never give away what you can charge for. I'd tell you who I learned that from, but she's now leading a respectable life with a rich husband and five little ones.

I can tell you another thing I've learned about show business—the importance of doing what's appropriate for your age. That's something it wouldn't hurt people outside of show business to think about, too.

How many times do you see fifty- and sixty-year-old

women wearing eye makeup that would be overdone on Halloween, and bulging out of their push-up bras and tight leather miniskirts? They think they look young and sexy. Just the opposite. What they look is older than they are and ridiculous. But these same women, with a nice hair style, a minimum of makeup, and clothes that are right for their figure, could be a pleasure to look at.

Some of you may never have heard of Blossom Seeley. She married Benny Fields, who you probably never heard of, either. They did a pretty good act together. But in her twenties, before Benny, Blossom was the hottest singer around. She was a knockout, with everything in the right places. One of her biggest hits was a number called "Toddling the Todello." Blossom's mistake was that she never allowed herself to grow old. When she was eighty she was still Toddling the Todello. At eighty you don't Toddle the Todello. You're lucky if you can toddle, period.

Now Sophie Tucker was different. She was known as the "Red Hot Mama." In her heyday she did a big job singing "If you can't see Mama every night, you can't see Mama at all . . ." She had the face and the figure to convince you that she didn't have to put up with any man who wouldn't do it her way. Years later, when she was an old, heavy Sophie Tucker, she still sang that song, but now she did it with a pistol in each hand. That was why you had to see Mama every night. If you didn't, one of those pistols just might go off. Smart lady.

I never thought much about the risk of not playing your age until after years of high ratings, our radio show suddenly went into a gradual slump. Something wasn't right. Everyone had a different answer: Gracie was too dumb, Gracie wasn't dumb enough, I didn't have enough to do, I had too much to do.

One night I was tossing in bed and it came to me. We were too old for what we were doing on the show. In real life we were a married couple. On the show Gracie would flirt with all the announcers. Our stories and jokes didn't go with our lives. So at the beginning of the next show I announced to our listeners that from then on we were going to play what we really were—George Burns and Gracie Allen, a married couple with two teen-age children. That's how we wrote the new scripts, and our ratings went back up and stayed up.

That taught me a good lesson. At seventy I adjusted material that I did when I was sixty, and at eighty what I did when I was seventy. Now at ninety-five I don't do anything that doesn't fit a ninety-five-year-old man.

Adjusting to their advancing age is tougher for the clowns and the zany comics than for the quieter comedians who depend on the humor of the lines they say. Jerry Lewis became a huge hit playing a moronic kid with that crazy voice and all those weird expressions. At his present age that doesn't work for him anymore. But every time he tries a more mature approach, his former image keeps getting in the way. It's the same with Pinky Lee and Soupy Sales. Ed Wynn couldn't be The Perfect Fool when he was pushing seventy.

On the other hand, Johnny Carson and I can go on forever. I already have. And with me, the adjustments were never that hard. My style of performing was always mature. I always wore a suit, smoked, reacted, no big takes, no big gestures. I always played it old. When I was young I was old. I was born old.

Every time Milton Berle sees me he says, "George, you look just like you looked thirty years ago—OLD!" Thirty years ago he said, "George, you look just like you looked thirty years ago—OLD!" But I've got the last laugh. I haven't had to change my way of working. All I have to do is come up with some different lines every few years.

There's something else I've learned about show business. You have to be very careful not to get sucked into undertaking something that isn't worth doing. If you're lucky, you've only wasted your time. If not, it could mean a failure that gives your career a major setback.

It's a business where the rewards for success can be very big, so when you're not selling yourself on something, there's always someone else who is trying to sell you on something. And where there's so much selling there's a lot of buying.

I've bought a few salamis that I sold myself, and a few more that others have sold me. I'll mention one of the latter, an hour TV show that the producers brought me all the way to Paris to appear in. It was taped in France and shown over here in America. It's too bad it wasn't the other way around. I was supposed to be showing three pretty French girls (and the viewing audience) the glamorous nightclubs of Paris.

The fact that the girls were French and Paris was their city, not mine, made the tour pretty ridiculous to start with. What they showed of the nightclubs was even more ridiculous. The bare bosoms in one club looked like the bare bosoms in the other clubs. What you saw of the clubs' acts and numbers never went over thirty seconds. And you couldn't tell which club you were in, but that didn't matter, because you didn't care.

Fortunately, I appeared only here and there in this fiasco. I was, as they said, the frosting on the cake. If there had been any more frosting, I wouldn't have come back, I would have stayed in France.

Everyone makes mistakes. The idea is to make as few as possible. But in show business even when you try to be objective, sometimes you can't help getting carried away. You shouldn't blame yourself, you have plenty of company.

Hollywood is known as the land of make-believe. And it is. But most of the make-believe takes place in the minds of the cast when the movies are being made. On the set there's never been a movie that wasn't another *Gone With the Wind* or *Best Years of Our Lives*.

I've been on those sets. Between takes everyone bubbles with enthusiasm. It's a three-month shooting schedule, but by the end of the first week victory is already in the air. On the chow line for lunch, gossip is out, predictions are in. "This one can't miss!" "All I know is it's the best thing I've ever been in!" "It's a blockbuster, I can feel it!" The director drops by to mingle with the troops. Everyone gathers around him. "How did yesterday's rushes go, C.B.?"

"Like gangbusters," he says. "Kids, I hate to tell

you, but we've got a hit on our hands." How many times have I heard that one before.

All through the shooting it couldn't be more up-beat. Everyone loves the picture—the producer, the director, the actors, the crew, the caterer, the guard at the gate. There's not a Doubting Thomas on the lot.

After the film has been edited, the producer holds a private screening for fifty of his friends. It's called a screening because he screens out anyone who might give an honest opinion of his movie. What are his friends going to tell him? That they hated it? Big surprise. His picture comes out with fifty votes of confidence.

When I'm at one of these screenings it may be only forty-nine and one half. I can't lie to my producer friends, but I don't want to knock their pictures, either. So when they proudly say to me, "How about that picture!" I just pat them on the back and say, "Yeah, how about it." If they say to me, "How did you like the picture?" I have a chance to go a little more overboard. I can say, "How did I like the picture? You gotta be kidding—how did I like the picture?" With answers like these I keep my self-respect without losing valuable job sources.

As important as it is to be objective about your opportunities, being objective about yourself is even more important. You can't go by what your friends tell you, or people who work for you. You have to be able to make your own honest evaluation of your strengths and weaknesses. When some performers look in the mirror they see what they want to see. The smart ones see the wrinkles.

Do you remember that hilarious army sit-com Phil Silvers used to do? Well, Phil once told me a story about the guy who played dopey-looking Doberman in that series. This fellow, whose real name was Maurice Gosfield, thought he had what it takes to be a stand-up comic. And somehow he got himself booked to do an hour in some little club fifty miles out of New York. And he made Phil promise to catch the act and come to his dressing room during intermission and critique the first half.

So it's show night, Phil's out there, and Gosfield is bombing. Nothing works. Not one laugh. It's a disaster. Intermission comes and like he promised, Phil goes backstage, thinking what can he say to the poor guy. He opens the dressing room door, Gosfield is sitting there fanning himself, and before Phil can open his mouth, he says, "Some first half, eh, Philsie—I'm home free."

That shows you how people can misjudge themselves. Fortunately, I've never had that problem. I've always been very objective about my comedic strength and weaknesses. The same goes for my singing. I know I haven't the voice to belt out songs. That's for Tony Martin or Tony Bennett. I could never rate with them. My singing is different. I'm in Frank Sinatra's class.

Like I say, you've got to be objective.

INTERLUDE

Nuggets of Wisdom

One of the great wits of all time was the person who called them Easy Payments.

—G. Burns

There are many ways to die in bed, but the best way is not alone.

—G. Burns

Interview with the Author
No. 1

Q: To what do you attribute reaching the age of ninety-five?
A: Last year I was ninety-four.

Q: What's your secret to enjoying old age?
A: I can't tell you. It's a secret.

Q: Do you think you're slowing up?
A: Not at all. A lot of people use a springboard to get into bed.

Q: Your doctor just said you have the heart of a lion. How do you feel about that?
A: I feel I should get a second opinion from my veterinarian.

Q: Why do you always take out young women?
A: Because I don't particularly enjoy the company of young men.

Q: If you were staying in a hotel, and a very voluptuous young woman came to your door and wanted to spend the night with you, how would you handle it?

A: I'd send her away out of respect for the two voluptuous young women already in the room.

Q: When was the first time you became interested in girls?

A: I'm not sure. I can only remember since I was three.

Q: Was there any time in your life that you considered yourself oversexed?

A: Only once. From March 3, 1914, to June 9, 1981.

Q: On a scale of one to ten, ten being best, how would you rate yourself as a singer?

A: I don't hear my number in there. Have you got anything from eleven to twenty?

Q: Is it true last week a twenty-year-old starlet was seen running her fingers through your hair?

A: True. I walked into my dressing room and caught her doing it.

Q: You're still considered an excellent dancer. How do you do it at your age?

A: I have pacemakers in my feet.

107

SEQUENCE VI

ON MY WAY HERE it occurred to me that you might be ready for a little change of pace, so this morning I'm just going to tell you some of my favorite stories. Good idea, isn't it. But I can just hear the nitpickers asking what a bunch of funny stories have to do with a book on wisdom. Well, they have a lot to do with it. It takes a wise person to know which story is funny and which isn't. You knew there had to be a connection. Would I ever drag something in if it didn't fit?

You'll notice I said I was going to tell you some of my favorite stories. I didn't say jokes. To me a joke is something that's made up. No matter who or what it's about, somebody sat down and thought it up to be funny. It's not something that really happened and turned out to be funny. To me that's a story. The other is a joke. With some people if a joke is long enough, it becomes a story. To me, long or short, if it was invented, it's a joke. If it really took place, it's a story.

There are good jokes and bad jokes, and good stories and bad stories. Good or bad, I don't happen to be a big fan of jokes. I seldom think they are as funny as the people telling them to me seem to think they are. Maybe that's partly because "Wait'll you hear this one!" is so often followed by a jab to my shoulder. I

111

don't enjoy being jabbed on the shoulder. Why do they do that?

And why do they laugh so hard at their punch line? Let me laugh. I'm hearing it for the first time. They've heard it twenty times that day because they've told it twenty times that day.

I hear my share of the jokes that make the rounds these days. I'm getting lots of shoulder jabs but very few laughs.

It must be because the ones I like the least are the ones that sweep across the country faster than the flu epidemic of World War I. They probably do almost as much damage. I'm talking about those two-line question and answer zingers that always need a target to aim at—a group, a race, a nationality, a profession. A typical example:

Question: How does a Jewish Princess call her family to dinner?
Answer: Okay, everybody into the car!

Same joke, different words:

Question: What does a Jewish Princess make for dinner?
Answer: Reservations.

After you've heard a few hundred of these, it turns out that the Jewish Princess doesn't cook or do housework, gets a lot of manicures, pedicures, and credit cards, but on the other hand, she's nothing in bed.

But she's not stupid. For stupid the same formula

"works" to ridicule the intelligence level of whatever race, minority, or nationality you want to pick on.

Question: How many Poles does it take to
change a light bulb?
(Mexicans)
(Italians)
(Blacks)
(Puerto Ricans)
Answer: One to hold the light and three to
turn the ladder.

That was good for a thousand variations. And let's not forget the lawyers:

Question: A dead lawyer and a dead snake are
lying in the street. What's the
difference between them?
Answer: There are skid marks in front of the
dead snake.

That'll teach them. During the Iraqi war last winter we called on the same formula, and it came through with gems like this:

Question: What did Saddam Hussein and his
father have in common?
Answer: They didn't withdraw in time.

Question: What's an Iraqi with a sheep under
each arm?
Answer: A pimp.

Question: What is a room with thirty-two Iraqi
women in it?

Answer: A perfect set of teeth.

You can see what all these jokes have in common—
meanness, ridicule, sarcasm, insensitivity—all the
things that a Mark Twain or Will Rogers somehow
managed to get along without. But that was my least-
funny-joke group. The one that's a little more amus-
ing has jokes that go on a few more lines and use
another clever formula:

Doctor: Mr. Jones, I have good news and bad
news for you.

Patient: What's the bad news?

Doctor: You have a week to live.

Patient: Oh gosh. Well, what's the good
news?

Doctor: I'm sleeping with my nurse.

And here's the other version:

Doctor: Mr. Jones, I've got bad news and
worse news for you.

Patient: Really? What's the bad news?

Doctor: You have twenty-four hours to live.

Patient: Oh no! What's the worse news?

Doctor: I was supposed to tell you yesterday.

At least these jokes aren't offensive, just a little
insensitive.

I'm not saying that there aren't any jokes that are

inoffensive and funny at the same time. But even those go in one ear of mine and out the other. For me, the funniest joke doesn't compare to a funny story. Here's my all-time favorite vaudeville story:

Wilton LaKye was one of the finest legitimate actors on Broadway, but he enjoyed playing vaudeville three or four weeks a year. He was headlining the Keith Theater in Cincinnati, and on the bill with him, opening the show, was a little dancing act, Dunbar and Dixon.

After Monday's rehearsal, LaKye went to the bar next door to have a drink. A few minutes later in came Dunbar and Dixon. When they saw this big star sitting there they went right over to him, and Dunbar said, "Mr. LaKye, we wanted you to know what a thrill it is for us to play on the same bill with you." LaKye said, "Thank you, boys."

Then Dixon said, "We would deem it an honor if we could buy you a drink."

LaKye said, "I'm sorry, boys, but I'd just as soon drink alone. I just got a wire saying that I lost my mother."

Dixon shook his head sadly and said, "We know just how you feel—our trunk is missing."

Maybe you'd have had to be in vaudeville to really appreciate that one.

This next story also concerns a pretty fair actor, John Barrymore. Barrymore got into a cab at Grand Central in New York City. The driver, who was Jewish and spoke with an accent, recognized him. He said, "Mr. Barrymore, I've seen you in a lot of movies." Barrymore said, "Good for you." The driver asked him what he was doing in New York, and Barrymore, in that grand manner of his, said, "I am here to appear in Shakespeare's *King Lear.*"

The driver was impressed. "King Lear," he said. "I've seen that a dozen times. I've seen it played by all the great actors—Jacob P. Adler, Boris Tomeshevsky, David Kessler, Maurice Schwartz." Then he thought a second and said, "Tell me something, Mr. Barrymore—do you think it'll go in English?"

Here's another vaudeville story. Novelty acts used to be very popular, and this one is about a fellow who worked with a chicken that danced on one leg. The act was called Jackie Davis and Chick Fowler. Chick Fowler was the fellow.

It wasn't a bad act, but Chick liked his booze. Every so often he'd pour some into a saucer for the chicken, and the chicken got to like it. It was hard enough for him to stand on one leg when he was sober, but when he was smashed it was murder. After a while they couldn't get a job.

One day I ran into Chick and I asked him how things were going. "Not good," he said. "Things are so rough that last night I pretty near ate my partner."

I said, "Chick, you wouldn't do a thing like that!"

He said, "Of course not. But I must admit I ate the leg he wasn't using!"

To me the two funniest performers visually were W. C. Fields and Ben Blue. All I had to do was look at Fields and I was ready to laugh. It was the same with

Ben Blue. No one could do Charlie Chaplin like Ben, with all those little moves. He sort of looked like Chaplin, only Charlie's eyes weren't crossed like Ben's.

One time Ben was in court getting a divorce. He didn't have a lawyer; he handled, or I should say mishandled, his own case. It got down to the money, and the judge mentioned some very large amounts that he felt Ben's wife deserved.

"Your Honor," Ben protested, "that's unfair for a man in my financial circumstances! If I have to give her that kind of money, I won't be able to put gas in my Duesenberg!"

The next time I saw him he was driving a Chevrolet.

Ben did one of the funniest bits I've ever seen on a stage. It was at the Palace, and he was doing that Chandu the Magician act of his. For one of his tricks he put a man into a big wicker box and then had the box raised so it hung about fifteen feet above the stage. Then he pointed a gun up at the box and shot through it. Everyone figured he'd open the box and nobody would be in it. Instead of that, blood started dripping down from the box onto the stage. Ben ignored it, just went on, paid no attention to the blood. For the rest of the act it kept dripping down. It was a riot.

When we were doing the Burns and Allen radio show, our bandleader was Artie Shaw, who was then married to Lana Turner. When we moved the show from New York to California, Artie had trouble with James Petrillo, the head of the musicians union. Petrillo wouldn't allow Artie's number-one trumpet player to leave New York, and Artie got very upset about it.

The day after we got to Los Angeles, I was on my way to the Brown Derby restaurant, and passing a newsstand I saw this big headline—LANA TURNER DIVORCES ARTIE SHAW. I was shocked.

Inside the Derby Artie was at the bar having a drink. I really felt bad for him, losing a beautiful girl like Lana. I put my arm around him, and I said, "Artie, don't take it too hard. Things like this happen to everybody." Artie looked at me and said, "To hell with Petrillo, I'll find a trumpet player out here."

With Artie first things came first.

Do you remember Major Bowes and his Amateur Hour on radio? "Round and round she goes, and where she stops nobody knows." Well, Gus Edwards was the Major Bowes of vaudeville. Gus would find talented kids, develop their acts, and send them around the vaudeville circuits. Big stars—Jessel, Cantor, Berle, Phil Silvers, Walter Winchell, and lots of others got their start with Gus Edwards. And they never forgot him.

One night about ten or fifteen years ago at the Friars Club, some little thing developed into a big argument with everyone shouting at each other, and from left field someone screamed at Georgie Jessel, "Your people killed Christ!" And Jessel said, "Well, I had nothing to do with it—I was with Gus Edwards."

That's a sample of the kind of lines Jessel could come up with. Others may have had more success, others may have done better with prepared material, but off the stage, in real situations, nobody had answers like Jessel. Very few have had as many wives, either. Mickey Rooney has. So has Artie Shaw. In Artie's case you can see why.

The wife of Georgie's life was Norma Talmadge. When she left him he found out that she was going with some doctor in Florida. Jessel went berzerk. He bought a gun, flew to Florida, went straight to Norma's hotel, knocked on the door, and when she opened it there was this doctor. Jessel took out his gun and took a shot at him. But the bullet went through the window and hit a gardener two blocks away who was bending over picking up a daisy.

When the gardener took Georgie to court, the judge asked, "Mr. Jessel, how is it possible for you to take a shot at someone ten feet away from you and hit a gardener two blocks away?"

And Jessel answered — — — —

What's that, Jack? He wants me now? I'm sorry, folks, that's my secretary, Jack Langdon, and Hal is going to have to take over for me again. My doctor had to cancel my appointment this afternoon, but if I get over to him right away, he can take me now. Let's go, Conrad! Hal, take over—

This is Hal again. And Jessel answered, "Your Honor, I'm an actor, I'm not Buffalo Bill." That's the end of the story. It would have been funnier to you coming from my boss. I don't have his delivery. I don't have his timing, his gestures, his voice, his cigar. I don't smoke cigars. I just inhale his.

George loves those Jessel stories. He's got

dozens of them. This one is like a follow-up to that one I just finished for him. One morning George was at his club, and he noticed that Jessel was already at the bar. After a few minutes he came over and said, "Georgie, I've been watching you—that's your third brandy, and it's only nine o'clock in the morning."

"Didn't you know?" Jessel said, "Norma Talmadge left me." George said, "But she left you thirty years ago." Jessel said, "I still miss her."

Funny line. It's too bad George couldn't have told it to you. Not George Burns, George Jessel. I'm not saying Jessel's delivery was funnier. I better not. But Jessel had something that made you laugh. I think it was his toupee. It did not fit him like a glove. It didn't fit him like a toupee, either. Jessel did hundreds of eulogies. Maybe he snatched it off a corpse before they closed the coffin.

I was just going to tell you another of George's favorites, but why should I do that? I can tell you mine. You'll love this one. Great joke. George likes stories, I like jokes:

This high school senior takes a summer job in his neighborhood grocery store. It's his first day, and a customer asks him for half a head of lettuce. He can't believe it. So he goes over to the owner and says, "Some jerk wants half a head of lettuce." As he says it he notices that same customer standing right next to them, so he quickly adds, "And this fine gentleman wants the other half." So they give the man his lettuce, and after he leaves, the owner says to the kid, "You think fast. That's a good quality. In fact, I've got another store and someday I may let you manage it."

"Great," the kid says. "Where is this store?" The owner says, "In Montreal." The kid says, "Montreal? All they have there is hookers and hockey players!" "Now hold on," the owner says, "I'll have you know my sister lives in Montreal." And the kid says, "Yeah? What team does she play for?"

You like that? George would say it's too long. I know he'd say that. After being with him for so long I think just like him. If I were a few years older, I could be him. Why am I standing here doing this? I'm late for the club. I'll miss my bridge game. Where's Conrad? Conrad? Where are you? Jack, if you see Conrad, tell him to wait, I have to go to the bathroom. . . .

INTERLUDE

Alan Berlin

Author taking oath that he has responded truthfully to questions of the interviewer.

Interview with the Author
No. 2

Q: Of all the characters in the Bible, Old and New Testament, who are your favorites?

A: King David, Delilah and Charlton Heston.

Q: Who's your favorite actor?

A: Jimmy Stewart. I like his pacing. It took him ninety-two years to be eighty-three.

Q: Do you know many of the young stars of today?

A: Yes. I've known Dolly Parton since she wore a training bra.

Q: Do you have a favorite one-man show?

A: Yes. Samson . . . he brought down the house. Thanks for asking. I haven't been able to use that line since Samson brought down the house.

Q: If you were really God and not just playing him, what changes would you make?

A: I'd revoke the Commandment about not coveting thy neighbor's wife. Why not keep it in the neighborhood?

Q: If some day after you leave us, if you ever do, and a movie is planned about your life, who would you like to play you?

A: Me. I'd come back for it.

Q: Have you ever been sorry you dropped out of grammar school?

A: Yes. When I think of what education has done for other people, I shudder to think of what a success I could have been.

Q: Have you ever done anything to further your formal education?

A: Yes. I've dated schoolteachers, but they all said they learned from me.

Q: Is there anything in your lifetime that you'd like to do that you haven't done?

A: Yes. Touch my left elbow with my left hand.

Q: You're pulling my leg.

A: That's another thing I haven't done.

Q: You must enjoy being called a living legend.

A: Why not? I won't enjoy being called a dead legend.

Q: I thank you for your time.

A: You're welcome, but I'd rather you paid me for it.

SEQUENCE VII

Alan Berliner

A hundred cookies and still no fortune.

DID YOU EVER HAVE one of those nights when some-thing was on your mind and you couldn't fall asleep? I had one last night. And do you know what was on my mind? A fortune cookie.

I don't understand fortune cookies altogether. I always thought fortune cookies were supposed to tell your fortune, to predict something in your future. "You are about to receive an offer you can't refuse." "Beware of a big office romance ahead, it may be a trap." I have yet to get one like that. I get compliments—"You have a way with children" or insults—"You have a tendency to be overly rigid."

Most of the ones I get have nothing to do with me, or anyone else. They are just some obvious thoughts about life in general. "The gift of true friendship is a gift to treasure." "It is when the night is darkest that day approaches." Who needs that? Just once I'd like to open a fortune cookie and read—"Your life is just beginning." That's a fortune cookie! Or maybe— "That oil well you gave up on is about to come in." Nothing wrong with that. I'd even settle for one that said, "Your next fortune cookie will tell your fortune."

Last night, after enjoying some very good Chinese take-out, I wasn't going to spoil it by opening my fortune cookie. But I couldn't resist, and there it was, another winner. "The highest knowledge is self-knowledge." By the time I got to bed I was over being annoyed and starting to think maybe that cookie was onto something. What's wrong with a little self-knowledge? I began asking myself questions I've never asked myself. It turns out I'm a subject that I haven't spent much time on. I don't know about self-analysis. Urinalysis I know. Self-analysis is not something you get the hang of overnight—even a sleepless one. So this morning, at the tender age of ninety-five, I'm sure there's still plenty I don't know about myself—but there are some things I do know.

I know that show business is my life. It always was and it always will be. Nothing holds my interest like show business, nothing excites me more. There's nothing I think or talk about as much. I love playing bridge. For the two hours I play it I forget everything else. But I couldn't play bridge all day. I could live without bridge. I would hate to have to live without show business.

When I'm working I'm happy. I don't have to go on vacations. Sitting around in some fancy resort in Hawaii or the Bahamas would bore me to tears. You couldn't get me on one of those six-week cruises, even with three weeks off for good behavior. Look, I'll go anywhere for a few weeks if I'm performing there. That's my kind of vacation. Have job, will travel. When I'm in London, Paris, Rome, Melbourne, I see the airport, the hotel I'm staying at, and the theater I'm working in. Sightseeing doesn't interest me. I don't applaud anything that can't applaud back.

There's another thing I know about myself. I don't

like change. Some people are always looking for something different. They keep changing jobs, changing cars, changing wives. If I ever left a job, it wasn't my doing. Change disturbs me. If Arlette gives me a new cereal for breakfast, my day is off to a bad start. If Daniel moves an ashtray in the living room or a glass in my bar, I may not know what he moved, but I sense that something is different. You might say I'm a creature of habit. I won't say it, because I don't see why I should call myself a creature.

If I can help it, nothing changes. Well, not nothing. I change my underwear, I change my socks, and once when the house was broken into I changed the locks on the doors. That upset me, too. It was a week before I could figure out how to get into my own house.

Whoever said, "If it ain't broke, don't fix it," is my kind of guy. I've lived in the same city for sixty-one years. I've belonged to the same club for fifty-seven years. I've had the same office for thirty-nine years. When I'm there I sit in the same chair, drink my tea from the same cup, smoke the same cigars, and write the same jokes. When I look across the room I see the same faces: Irving, Jack, and Hal. Conrad has only been with me a few years, but if he keeps laughing, he'll be there as long as I am.

That's me. If something works, I stay with it. I was married to Gracie for thirty-eight wonderful years. If she were still here, it would be sixty-five.

There's something I know I'm not. I'm not insecure. I don't think I ever was. I've never felt nervous walking out on a stage, and I've never lain awake nights worrying that my career was over.

And if it's up to me I'll live here another fifty-three years.

Insecurity is the curse of show business. I've never known an actor who wasn't insecure. And comedians are worse than actors. Why didn't that punch line get a laugh? Maybe I'm losing it. Maybe I'm too clean. Maybe I'm too dirty. Maybe I should stop copying Robin Williams. Maybe I should copy someone else.

They try to hide their fears by looking confident. And if they do have any confidence that isn't just on the surface, it's easily shattered. When I was playing at the Riviera Hotel in Las Vegas this year I went to see a stand-up comedian I know who was appearing at another hotel on the Strip. He did a good show, and by the time I got to his dressing room he was already holding court for his friends and fans. "How about that show!" he crowed. "I was never better. What a performance! I was sharp! I was with it! I had that audience eating out of my hand!" So just in fun I said, "I was out front, and I didn't think you were that good." He said, "The band loused me up." In two seconds his confidence was gone.

It's different now, but when I was floundering around in vaudeville no one had more reason to be insecure than I did. But I didn't think I was a flop. I thought the audience was. If I got canceled, so what? I wasn't worried. And in those days money wasn't something I had, it was something I owed. I didn't have enough to buy food. There were times when I had to live for weeks on what the audience threw at me. To this day I can't stand tomatoes. It's funny, I still like coconuts.

There's something else I know about myself, but I don't know how I should put it. I don't know if I should

E

A standing ovation and it's not even payday. Left to right: my secretary, my writer, my driver, and my manager.

say that I'm not good at showing my feelings, or that I'm good at not showing my feelings. That's because I'm not sure whether this is a good or bad quality.

Whatever it is, I'm stuck with it. I've read reviews that applaud my underplayed, laid-back style of acting. I've got news for them. That's not acting—that's me.

It's not that I don't have feelings. When Gracie died I cried a lot. At Jack Benny's funeral I got up to give my eulogy, and I wasn't five words into it before I choked up and had to sit down. I think that was the only time in my life that I showed emotion in public. With Gracie the tears were private.

There's something that makes me keep my emotions in check. Maybe I have British blood in me. I should have asked my mother about that. There were twelve of us kids, but my father spent lots of nights reading the Talmud.

It goes beyond holding back my emotions. I can't rave about things, can't gush over people. Words like gorgeous, magnificent, super-talented, tremendous, colossal don't come out of my mouth. If Bert Parks still hosts beauty pageants, he doesn't have to worry about me, I couldn't do his job.

Some people can let it all hang out. On the old "Tonight Show," Jack Paar was an emotional basket case. He was either doubled over laughing or on the verge of tears. During one of his shows he went into a tirade because the network censors wouldn't let him say "water closet," and then stomped off the stage, never to return. Johnny Carson is just the opposite. No one can tell what goes on under that grin of his. He may have some British blood in him, too.

I even have trouble being serious. When I'm not before the public I can be serious for a minute or so. I can be serious if a role I'm playing requires it. But when I appear as George Burns I'm very uncomfortable playing it straight. Maybe that's because I don't think people expect that from me. I think they expect me to be funny.

When I'm interviewed I rarely give a serious answer to a question. If I'm asked what I think of the young comedians, I'll say, "You mean Milton Berle, Bob Hope, Henny Youngman—those kids will do fine." I don't go into a big discussion about the abilities or the problems of young comedians.

It's the same with the commercials I do. Sometimes the ad agency will send over a straight commercial. I want to make it funny. If the client, for his own reasons, wants a straight commercial, then I'm ready to turn it down. My manager will say, "Bob Hope and Bill Cosby are comedians, and I've seen them do lots of commercials without a single laugh in them." I say, "Then let them get Hope or Cosby." I feel strongly about that. I must. Some of those commercials I've turned down would have paid a fortune.

When it comes to revealing my feelings, maybe I hold back too much. When you're my age maybe it's time to let go a little. I realize that people would like to know what I really feel about reaching this stage of my life. But I can't let my hair down. I have enough trouble keeping it on. With me it has to come out funny or with an attempt to be funny.

Maybe someday I'll be able to open up more. In the meantime let me give you the words of a song that I

always do in my stage show. It's called "Old Bones,"
and maybe I keep singing it because it says for me what
I can't seem to say for myself. I promise not to try to
top it with something funny.

> Old bones
> Inside an old raincoat
> Old bones
> Inside of old shoes
> Old friends from the hotel
> Come by to wish me well
> And keep me up to date
> On all the good news.
> Sometimes I have me a whiskey
> And I fall asleep in my chair
> Old bones don't move so fast
> Like they did once in the past
> Now if I have to run
> I simply don't go.
> But I love life
> I'd like to do it again
> Though I might not be
> Much more
> Than I've ever been
> Just to have the chance
> To turn back the hands
> And make my life begin
> Oh yeah
> I'd like to do it again
> Oh yeah
> I'd like to do it again.

I kept my promise.

INTERLUDE

Nuggets of Wisdom

There are two kinds of cruises—pleasure and with children.

—G. Burns

A young mind in a healthy body is a wonderful thing. Especially for an old man with an open night.

—G. Burns

The Dumbest Dumb Animals

Centipede

He can't even learn to dance . . . he's got two hundred left feet.

Hummingbird

It's about time he learned the lyrics.

Frog

When's the last time you heard of one knowing how to turn back into a prince?

Camel

He's proud of being able to go for days without a drink. In some circles he'd be run out of town for that.

Worm

He's been known to fall in love with his other end.

Turkey

He knows he's going to get it in the neck in November
. . . why doesn't he ever take off in October?

Anteater

Enough said right there.

Pit Bulldog

He's too stupid to know he's man's best friend.

Moose

He's got that big hatrack and doesn't wear a hat.

Zebra

He's so dumb he doesn't know whether he's dark
with white stripes or white with dark stripes. What
can you expect from something that's a half-horse and
a half-ass?

SEQUENCE VIII

I GUESS IT'S TIME to give some advice. I've been putting it off as long as I can. The only thing I like less than giving advice is getting it. Who am I to give advice? I'm a country singer. There are people who get paid to give advice. Professionals. And I'm not so sure about them, either.

Psychiatrists spend their whole day straightening out their patients' lives. When you come into their office, the first thing they do is put you down on a couch, and for the next hour they listen to whatever comes to your mind. That's not quite right. The first thing they do is turn the meter on.

Look, if they can straighten you out, they're entitled to whatever they can charge. But how is it I once read that these experts at making unhappy people happy are the leading group when it comes to committing suicide? Now, I'm not saying that's true. I'm only telling you what I read. And what I read may be totally wrong. The last thing I need is psychiatrists getting mad at me. They might stop seeing my relatives.

Then there are the experts who tell you how to bring up your kids. The child psychologists. I happen to know one. He's a very nice man. I've been to his house—once. I have never seen a seven-year-old carry on like that son of his. If he were mine, he'd never make it to eight. He screamed, he ran through the house, got the dog crazy, pulled chairs over, including the one I was sitting in, shot me with his water pistol, and got ink all over my shirt. Outside of that he was very well behaved.

Well, I can't stall any longer. They tell me a book of wisdom has to give advice. So here it comes, whether I like it or not.

What should we start with? Money? Why not. Here's my advice to you on money—make it. And when you make it, spend it. Buy things. That's what money is for, not to prop up tables that tilt. And if you feel like gambling with it, go ahead, have a good time. Forget that stuff about saving for a rainy day. Joe E. Lewis, the great saloon performer, blew fortunes at the racetrack, but he didn't care. He used to say, "They tell me to save for a rainy day. But with my luck I'll save, it'll never rain, and I'll be stuck with all that money."

And don't believe that old wives' tale about money not buying happiness. (Why is it always an old wives' tale? Don't old husbands have tales? If we're going for equality of the sexes, let's have it both ways.) Money buys lots of things, including more money. It doesn't have to buy happiness—it buys diamonds and furs, fancy cars, yachts, mistresses—and they make you happy. But then who knows? Are the people who have those things happy? Maybe they just look happy.

Money definitely has its place. But don't make being rich your life's goal. Many have done just that, probably even more than have made being poor their life's goal.

148

These are decisions that everyone has to make for himself—or herself—shame on me! If you feel that amassing great wealth is really important to you, then go for it. No one can stop you, except maybe a federal judge or two.

If I have to give my advice, and it seems that I do, I would tell you that accumulating money is fine, but don't overdo it. As Joe E. Lewis said, "Is a man with $10,000,000 happier than a man with $9,000,000?" He couldn't say that now. Today he'd have to say, "Is a man or woman with $10,000,000 happier than a man or woman with $9,000,000?" That's enough for Joe E. Lewis. And that's enough for money.

How am I doing so far? You want more of this? Okay, here are a few things for you younger people to take to heart. Let's start with a situation a lot of you may find yourselves in. You've got a job, maybe your first, it pays good money, but your boss is taking advantage of you or doing other things that you resent. What to do? I say don't hold it in. Go straight to your boss and tell him exactly what you think of him. That way you'll gain his respect and also get fired. But when that happens you'll not only be out of a job that was making you uptight, but you'll have the satisfaction of knowing you have the respect of the man who fired you.

Some of you may be college football stars with offers to turn professional while you still have a year or two of school left. Stay in school. You owe it to your teammates. You'll have a chance to bring your grades up to a "D," and you may even make more money playing for your school than the pros would pay you.

And here's something for you kids who are in love. Don't rush into marriage. Resist all that pressure from your peers and live together for a while. If a baby comes along that looks like you, and you want to keep it, then you can get married. And remember— marriage is a two-way street. I don't know what that means, but remember it.

What else? Oh yes, here's my advice to you young comedians—live to be old comedians. I don't see how you can go wrong with that.

Since comedy is my field I've had occasion to give advice personally to dozens of young comedians, like Robin Williams, Billy Crystal, David Letterman, Martin Short, John Candy. Those aren't the ones I gave advice to. I would have, but they never asked for my advice.

I did give advice to Sam Newman, Ben Higby, Hank Henderson, Artenio Ball and Teddy Murphy. When they came to me for suggestions, I didn't hold back. I told them everything I knew. I even showed them how I work. I'm not going to do that anymore. It's been four or five years since I advised those kids, and to this day I haven't had a word of thanks from a single one of them.

Let's see. I had a thought for another group. Oh yeah, all you teenagers out there. The big mistake you're making is that you listen to all that bad advice from kids your own age. You should listen to your parents. They're entitled to give you bad advice.

That's the whole trouble, there's too much bad advice floating around. That's nothing new. There's always been advice that wasn't worth listening to.

How long have you been hearing, "Don't hit a man when he's down?" What kind of advice is that? If you're going to hit a man, that's when you hit him. What should you do, hit him when he's up and can hit you back?

And there's so much advice that's contradictory. Don't marry for love—don't marry for money. It's either one or the other. What's wrong with marrying for love? My mother never told my sisters not to marry for love. She didn't care what they married for as long as they got married. She didn't even mind when they didn't marry doctors. If I were you, I'd forget don't marry for love and go with don't marry for money. Borrowing it can be less painful.

I've got to tell you, a lot of advice that people have assumed is brilliant never did make sense to me— "Don't burn your bridges behind you." In the first place, why are they "your" bridges? How many people do you know who own bridges? But all right, say they are your bridges. I know a man who burned his clothing store and a few who burned their restaurants, but I have yet to meet a man who burned his bridge. And why are they telling you not to burn the ones behind you? Does that mean it's okay to burn the ones in front of you? I don't know about you, but I've come to quite a few rivers I wouldn't want to have to swim across.

And what about "Make hay while the sun shines"? Why hay? I don't like hay. I like martinis. Why can't I make a martini while the sun shines? And whether it's hay or a martini, why do I have to make it while the sun shines? I've made some excellent martinis when it was cloudy.

"Build a better mousetrap and they'll beat a path to your door." Now that one's different. It's longer. But to me it makes no more sense than the others. Why would I want mice beating a path to my door? I have enough trouble with cemetery-lot salesmen. Besides, it's not everyone who can build a better mousetrap. I couldn't build a worse mousetrap. Before I bother with mousetraps, let me figure out how to work the wipe-off on my answering machine, or pry an airport baggage cart loose from that rack they're jammed into.

Right now I don't know what advice makes sense to me. All I know is that there's too much of it. The best advice of all may be no advice. That's not my line. It's from another fortune cookie.

INTERLUDE

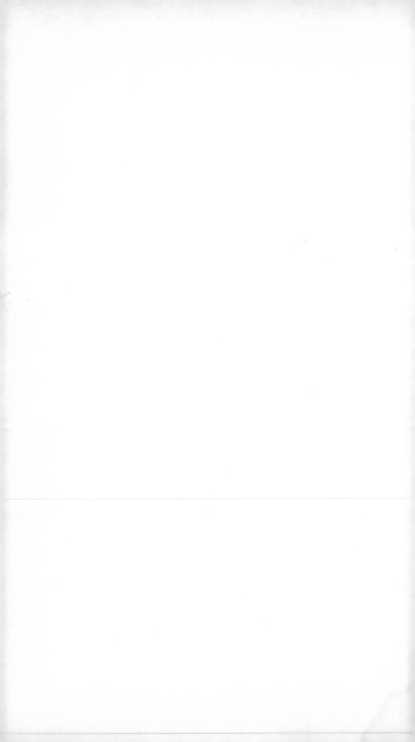

Some Signs That Old Age Might Be Creeping Up on You

When you like to be in crowds because they keep you from falling down.

When your only party of the past year was to celebrate the twelfth return of your seven-year itch.

When the parts that have arthritis are the parts where you feel the best.

When your favorite section of the newspaper is "25 Years Ago Today."

When your sex drive shifts from cruise control to neutral.

When a big evening with your friends is sitting around comparing living wills.

When your knees buckle but your belt won't.

When your clothes go into the overnight bag so you can fill the suitcase with your pills.

When you resent the annual swimsuit issue of *Sports Illustrated* because there are fewer articles to read.

When your idea of a change of scenery is looking to the left or right.

When somebody you consider an old-timer calls you an old-timer.

When you find you're no longer worried about being involved in a paternity suit.

SEQUENCE IX

I HAVE BAD NEWS and good news for you. The bad news is that I have a little more advice to give you. The good news is that what I'm now going to tell you are the things that I really believe, not like all that silly stuff I said yesterday. What happened then was that I started getting laughs from my little group in the office, and when I have an audience I don't know when to stop. But that was yesterday. As Ed Wynn used to start off his "Texaco Hour" in that cracking voice of his—"Graham, tonight the show is going to be different!" See, this is already different. Yesterday I quoted Joe E. Lewis, today it's Ed Wynn.

Let me clear up something here. This book has not been without real advice. It's there, sprinkled in with all the observations about myself, about show business, about people old and young, and about life in general.

Before you can make observations, you need to have a point of view. And to have a point of view you need knowledge and experience, also known as wisdom. It takes wisdom to make the observation that there's wisdom in knowing the right amount of advice to give. (I must have gone past the fourth grade.)

If it's all advice, you end up with one of those How-To books: *How to Save Your Marriages, How to Repair*

Your Yacht, How to Remake Your Body, How to Cut Your Toenails. I didn't want this to be a How-To book. On the other hand I don't want it to be a What-For book either.

Now that I got all that off my chest, pay close attention, because this may be the best advice you're going to get from me. Fall in love with what you are doing for a living. That's so important that I'm going to repeat it. Fall in love with what you are doing for a living. If you love your work, you've got it made. If you don't, you've got a very big problem.

I see people who go to jobs every day that they can't stand. Not just blue collar workers, but people who found out too late that they got into the wrong profession. They're the ones who support the antacid business. They suffer from indigestion, fatigue, tension headache, back pain, constipation—everything, including the heartbreak of psoriasis.

I feel sorry for them. I couldn't live every day of my life like that. I always said I'd rather make $200 a week doing something I love than a million dollars doing something I hate. I haven't said it for a few years, so make that $400 a week and two million. If it's not a funny line, at least let it be up-to-date.

Fortunately, I don't have to settle for the $400. I make out all right, and I'm doing what I love. That's now. But how I was doing never made that much difference. When I was in small-time vaudeville and couldn't get jobs, I was happy because I was out of work in a business that I loved. And when the jobs I got didn't last and I had to keep trying to get new ones, I was still happy. I was in action. I was moving. With acts like mine I had to keep moving.

Today it's still fun, still just as exciting. At my age it's pretty nice to wake up in the morning and be able to look forward to what you're going to do the rest of the day. Someday you can have that feeling, too. It's simple. Just find yourself some work that isn't work to you.

Here's something else that I highly recommend to you. If you really believe in something, don't let anyone talk you out of it. There's always someone to say, "Forget it." "It won't work." "You're out of your mind." Sometimes everyone says that. Once in a while they're right. But you have to go with what you think. It may involve big sacrifices on your part. It may mean fighting with people you'd rather not fight with. Then again, it may mean fighting with your wife or your husband.

Even if you go down in flames, it'll be easier for you to live with yourself than if you gave up. I know what you're thinking—that's easy for me to say. You're right, talk is cheap—except when it comes from your lawyer. I'll admit something else. I'm no big hero. If I could have cast someone to play me in a movie, I would have picked John Wayne. I think he could have played me even better than that cowardly little Mexican bandit I suggested him for.

But when it came to putting up or shutting up, there have been quite a few times when I didn't shut up, and I've never regretted any of them.

A short time after the Burns and Allen Show went

from radio to television, I had what I thought was a brilliant idea. Our main set was a normal living room, but with most of the front exterior brick wall cut away so you could see inside. From time to time on every show I would step over the bricks to get outside the room, make some hilarious comments directly to the audience, then go back inside and we would pick up the plot from where I had left it. It was a good device. It worked great in the play *Our Town,* which I adapted it from. I'm glad I thought of that word. It sounds so much better than "stole."

My new idea was to place a television set in another room. At various times during the show I would be in that room, the TV set would be on, and the camera would shoot me watching Gracie and the rest of the cast on the TV screen. This was never done before, and it had great possibilities. I would see Gracie planning some scheme to fool me, and when I would rejoin Gracie and the others, the fact that I knew what was going on, and she wouldn't know that I knew, would make for all sorts of funny twists.

My writers and I came up with a great script, and I couldn't wait to go into rehearsal with it. Then the bubble burst. I was summoned to a meeting with our sponsor and his ad-agency representative. The agency man spoke first. He said that speaking for himself he was sorry to tell me that my idea wouldn't work, that it wasn't plausible, and that it would destroy the believability of all our shows.

I thought to myself, "What does he know?" Out loud I thanked him for his opinion, and added that I was sorry to have to tell him that I still liked my idea and wanted to do it. The sponsor then said loudly and firmly, "I'm in total agreement with him!" and he wasn't pointing at me. This was my sponsor talking now. I thought to myself, "What do I know?"

But then I stopped talking to myself and started talking to him. I tried to explain why my idea was such a good one, but he kept shaking his head sideways, not up and down. The more I talked the more shaking I got. I began to feel my dander coming up, and I hadn't felt that for years. Finally I told him flat-out that if I couldn't do my idea, he'd better find another show to replace us, at which point the meeting was adjourned. I could have changed my mind but I didn't. I had meant every word I said, and I was ready to face the consequences. Fortunately, I didn't have to. The next day I was told I could do it my way. That's the way we did it, it worked out great and became one of the most distinctive and talked-about features of our show.

If Norman Lear and Bud Yorkin hadn't stood up to the CBS brass, their show "All in the Family" would have died before it was born. After it had been turned down by ABC, CBS had given the go-ahead, but the week it was to be aired, William Paley and everyone else at CBS went into panic. They insisted that all of Archie Bunker's racist and ethnic slurs be softened or eliminated.

Norman and Bud refused. Without those lines there was no Archie Bunker. On air day Norman announced that if the censor took out one of their lines, they would cancel the show. "All in the Family" went on as written, and after a few months when it looked like the network might have been right, the public got over their initial shock, the ratings zoomed, and "All in the Family" became one of the most successful shows in the history of television. Needless to say, Norman and Bud haven't done badly either.

I could name you dozens of the biggest movies that were turned down by some or all of the major studios. They would never have made it to the screen if someone hadn't had the faith and the determination to keep pushing them. I happen to know about show business, but I hear the same kind of stories from people in other businesses.

They all teach the same lesson: If you really think you're right, stick to your guns no matter how much opposition or ridicule you have to put up with. As Gracie said on one of our shows, "They all laughed at Joan of Arc, but she didn't care. She went right ahead and built it."

I've saved this piece of advice for the last. Don't retire. I have very strong feelings on this subject. Are you surprised to hear that? If you are, then it would be news to you that I smoke cigars.

I don't believe in retirement. For me or anyone else. I used to go around giving all the arguments against it. I don't have to do that anymore. I don't have to say a word. If I thought retirement was a good move, would I still be working at the age of ninety-five? I could have retired thirty years ago. So it's not as though I haven't had time to change my mind.

Most of the people I know are connected with show business. The happiest are the ones that are still working. The saddest are the ones who are retired. Most of them are not retired by choice. It's either due to poor health or lack of job offers. Everyone who isn't in poor health would love a little work. A lot of work would be even better.

Very few performers retire on their own. Harry Lauder, the world-famous Scotch entertainer, went on a big Farewell Tour when he was in his sixties. It was a huge success. Everyone came to say goodbye to Harry. The next year he was back with his bagpipes and stingy jokes—on another Farewell Tour. That went over just as big. From then on, until it was really farewell for Harry, he took his annual Farewell Tour to Europe, Australia, and Japan. Those Farewell Tours made up one of the most successful periods of his career.

Five or six years ago Frank Sinatra announced his retirement. It made headlines all over the world. No more singing. He was just going to relax and enjoy himself. That lasted about six months. You know how busy he's been since then. This year he's going around the world doing one-nighters with Steve Lawrence and Eydie Gormé. It's billed as his Farewell Tour. Wanna bet?

I couldn't retire if I wanted to. I've become an example to too many senior citizens. They figure if I can keep going, so can they. If I quit, I'd be letting them down. Well, they don't have to worry, I'm not quitting. I'm going to stay in show business until I'm the only one left.

A few weeks ago I was in the waiting room of one of my doctors, and the man sitting next to me seemed to want to talk. I would have talked to him even if he hadn't told me he was a big fan of mine. I don't have to know people to talk to them. My mother never told me not to talk to strangers. Gracie's mother did. That's what she said in that vaudeville opening of ours that I told you about—the one where she's at the side of the stage kissing the man, and then says to me, "Who was that?" My next line was, "You don't know?" And she said, "No. My mother told me never to talk to strangers."

Back to my doctor's office and the stranger sitting next to me. I could see right away that he had a nice personality, he was obviously intelligent, and he listened to everything I had to say. I got to like him so much that when the nurse called me, I said to him, "Ed, before I go inside, I'm going to tell you something you'll thank me for someday. You look about sixty or sixty-five, so if you're thinking of retiring, don't. Stay the way you are—young-looking, bright, alert. If you retire, you'll sit around with nothing to do. You'll be bored to tears. Your muscles will get soft, your brain will get soft. You'll look and act like a man of eighty. Now promise you'll take my advice."

He said, "You're too late, I retired thirteen years ago."

I was shocked. "You gotta be kidding," I said. "If you retired thirteen years ago, that would make you seventy-eight. You don't look seventy-eight."

"I'm not seventy-eight," he said, "I'm eighty-three. I didn't retire at sixty-five, I retired when I was seventy."

I said, "Then why did you let me keep going like I did?"

He said, "Because I'm bored. That's the one thing you said about retirement that was on the nose."

At least I was right about something. How about that? I had to find the one guy that retirement wasn't so bad for. Well, it's not for me, that's for sure. But I suppose it wouldn't hurt to start thinking about it. Maybe I'll do that in another twenty or thirty years.

INTERLUDE

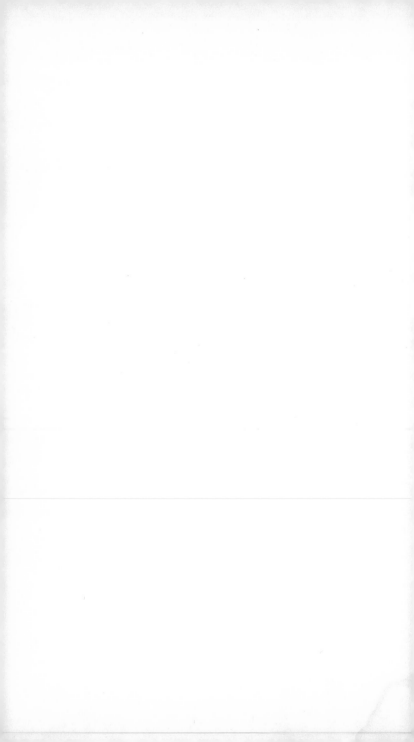

Nuggets of Wisdom

What the world needs is less people making more people.

—Anonymous

Too many people think they have an open mind when it's just vacant.

—Anonymous

If the shoe fits, wear it.

—Anonymous

Author's Note:

I'm sure Anonymous tried his best on that last one, but he stopped too soon. I would have said if the shoe fits, wear it, but not when you're in the shower. Come to think of it, I like his better.

Five Ways to Improve the World

1. Make a pill-bottle top that can be opened in time to avoid calling 9-1-1.

2. Have target practice for newsboys who toss your paper everyplace but where they're supposed to, like on your roof, in your pool, or in the sprinklers while they're on.

3. Design a mailbox that's chemically treated to make junk mail self-destruct.

4. Require doctors and dentists to pay the extra parking fees you incur because of the hour or two they kept you waiting.

5. Bring back vaudeville.

Nothing beats the convenience of having your morning paper delivered.

SEQUENCE X

WHEN I STARTED THIS book I wasn't sure that I had enough wisdom to get me to the finish. It would be embarrassing if I ran out somewhere along the way. There's no wisdom station where you can drive in and say, "Fill me up." The Auto Club's no help. But I guess I didn't have to worry. Although it's going to be close, it looks like I'm going to make it.

You know by now that I never got past the fourth grade. I've pleaded guilty to that several times already. But of all the performers from my generation, who finished school? I can't think of one. Jolson, Cantor, Durante, Jessel—they were all grade-school dropouts. Jack Benny went all the way to the ninth grade. But Jack didn't grow up with us on New York's East Side, he grew up in Waukegan, Illinois. We played stickball in the street, Waukegan kids played baseball in parks and wore uniforms. We played harmonicas, Jack played the violin. I think that's what he was playing.

What Jack lacked in formal education he made up by reading books. I never learned much from books. I've written more than I've read. Jessel read lots of books. He wouldn't have said it that way. Jessel would have said he was an inveterate reader. He loved big words and fancy phrases. Those eulogies that he would do at the drop of a body were something to hear.

Laying a colleague to rest, he would say, "We who are gathered here in this mossy glen, basking in the warm and lugubrious presence of this master of comedy, this cornucopia of wit, we know that the tears we shed are tears of joy for the fond memories with which he has endowed us." Imagine his "phraseology" if he had gone to high school.

Most of today's comedy stars are well educated. John Candy, Billy Crystal, Jay Leno, David Letterman, Steve Martin, Robin Williams all went to college. Bill Cosby, Chevy Chase, and Bob Newhart are university graduates. The comedians I grew up with didn't know what a campus looked like. The only time they were at Harvard, Princeton, or Yale was to pick up the honorary degrees they were awarded later in their lives.

I got one of those myself in 1988 from the University of Hartford. They made me a Doctor of Humanities. It was the first degree I was ever given. I told them how excited I was to receive such an honor, and then I said, "Now that I'm a doctor I can save a fortune. If I ever have to have open-heart surgery again, I can do it myself." They wanted to take my diploma back. I was joking. I know the difference between a Doctor of Humanities and a medical doctor. A medical doctor makes more money. They let me keep my diploma. They even let me keep the cap and gown. I wear it whenever I read the editorial page of the morning paper. It hasn't been out of the closet for months.

Look, a formal education is great. I'd be the last to knock it. But without it, we survived. It was trial-and-

Steve Laschever

Yes, that Doctor of Humanities is really me. I'm saving the black gown in case I'm appointed to the Supreme Court.

error—just like with our acts. If a line or a joke worked, you kept it in. If it didn't, you threw it out. Sometimes they threw you out with it.

Experience was our teacher. And most of us got pretty good grades. You learned that you had to be on your toes, that you had to make your own breaks.

One day during the lean years, I was sitting in a small-time booking office, waiting for something to happen, and I heard the secretary tell the agent that the Myrtle Theater had an opening the next night for Maurice Valenti and His Wonder Dog. I told the agent I was Maurice Valenti, he made the booking for me, I went out and found myself a dog, and the next night I walked out on the stage with the dog under my arm and sang my songs. In the middle of my act the dog did his act—twice. It ruined my finish, I couldn't do my sand dance.

That one didn't work out too good. Neither did some of the others. But something must have worked or I couldn't have had the career I've had.

I can't believe it's been eighty-eight years since I started singing for pennies with the PeeWee Quartet at the age of seven. If I'd have known show business was going to be this good to me, I wouldn't have waited so long to get into it.

Every life has a few major events that change its direction. Without question the biggest turning point of my life was Gracie Allen. Until she came along, I was going no place. No matter what I tried the audience disliked it. I got so used to being disliked I thought I was doing well. I didn't know what failure was. How could I? I never had any success to compare it to.

The good things for me started with Gracie, and for the next thirty-eight years they only got better. It wasn't a marriage that we had to work at. I made her laugh, and when she was around I was happy. And then one day she wasn't around anymore. It still doesn't seem right that she went so young and that I've been given so many years to spend without her.

Everything has a price. With old age it's losing so many of the people who mean the most to you. At my club I always had lunch at the same table. Besides myself, there was Jack Benny, Al Jolson, Georgie Jessel, the Marx Brothers, the Ritz Brothers, Lou Holtz and Danny Kaye—each one trying to be the funniest. They're all gone. I'm the only one left. I guess that makes me the funniest.

What can you do? When the guy knocks on your door you have to go. When he knocks on my door, I'm not going to answer it.

You have to take each day as it comes, and be thankful for who's left and for whatever you can still do. I've got my daughter, Sandy, and my son Ronnie, seven grandchildren and five great-grandchildren. They keep me busy, and so does my work. Without that I'd be lost. That's why I'm so grateful that after all these years there's not only still a demand for me, but I seem to have more fans than ever. I guess it's my luck that whatever it is I've got, I've had it the longest.

I have to say it's been quite a career so far. I've had nothing but fun and more than my share of recogni-

Conrad

It's pretty lonely these days at that Hillcrest round table.

tion. Countless awards. Hundreds of plaques. Keys to dozens of cities. I still don't know what those keys are for. There never was a city I couldn't get into. Just some I had trouble getting out of.

You can walk on three stars of mine on Hollywood Blvd. My footprints and cigar print are in cement at Grauman's Chinese Theater. I've had several sandwiches named after me. George Burns Road now borders Cedars-Sinai Medical Center. It crosses Alden Drive. They're thinking of changing Alden Drive to Allen Drive, and inviting me to the ceremony dedicating that intersection. I've already got my opening line: "Well, here I am back on Burns and Allen."

For a performer the biggest satisfaction is having the respect and approval of fellow performers. Here in Hollywood we have our own way of showing that. We give "Roasts." As the honored guest at several of these affairs, I've had the pleasure of sitting there in my tuxedo and hearing myself called: the sweetheart of the Stone Age; the man who embarrassed everyone at the Last Supper by asking for seconds; a man old enough to be his own father; a man who told Betsy Ross, "Personally I feel the pattern's a little busy, but let's run it up the flagpole and see if anyone salutes it." That's the praise I can repeat.

Early this year my club gave a big dinner in honor of my ninety-fifth birthday. The dais was loaded with talent. One of the first speakers was Irving Brecher, the creator-writer of "The Life of Riley" and the director of many fine movies. He paid me such a beautifully expressed compliment that I'm going to quote him exactly as he worded it.

Not everyone gets a road named after him. Part of my deal is that I have to stand here like this for an hour every day.

Burt Harris

Part of the gang at my birthday dinner. Standing: Barry Mirkin and Red Buttons. Seated: Chris Lemmon, Jack Lemmon, the Birthday Boy, Milton Berle, Jan Murray, Larry Gelbart, and Danny Thomas.

Burt Harris

The dais for my ninety-fifth birthday dinner. By the time they all got through speaking, I was ready for my ninety-sixth.

He said, "What is so unusual about our guest of honor this evening is that in a profession that is so frenetically competitive—where the pressure to make it big is so intense that often friends turn on one another—George Burns does not have a single enemy. They all died."

It's not often that you get to hear something that nice about yourself. But then I should have expected that from Irving. He's one of my closest friends.

Irving was right. This is a competitive business. It's not easy to get ahead. And you can't do it alone. I've had lots of help along the way, and I've had help with this book, too. I think it's time for a few thanks.

First, I should mention my literary agents, Arthur and Richard Pine. It all starts with them. When they get an idea for a book for me to do, they check it out with Phyllis Grann to see if it's something G. P. Putnam would want me to do. If she's enthused, they contact my manager. If he's enthused, they have numerous conference calls to hammer out the details. When everything is settled they tell me what they're all enthused about. I get off easy. All I do is write the book.

Incidentally, Phyllis insists that the Pines deserve credit for the title of this book. She says they came up with it, not her as I said in the Foreword. Sorry, fellows, it's too late. If I rewrite the Foreword now, it'll be a Backward.

Now for my manager. Irving Fein has had two clients in his entire managing career—Jack Benny and myself. I guess he dislikes change as much as I do. I've paid him lots of compliments. In one book I wrote that Irving Fein is the most generous person I know—there isn't a single charity that he doesn't insist I contribute to. I have another compliment for him. Irving has three qualities I value most in a manager: he's honest, he has good judgment, and he always tries to do what's in my best interest. My only complaint is that sometimes he thinks he's the only one who knows what's best for me. I know what's best for me—Irving Fein.

This is the fifth book Hal Goldman has helped me write. So there's nothing I can say about him that I haven't already said, for which I'm sure he's grateful. Actually, Hal is too good a writer to just help me. I keep telling him he should write a book on his own. And it doesn't have to be about my life. For a change it can be about his life. I even gave him the title—"My Life Writing for George Burns." What more can I do?

I have one other writer to thank—Seaman Jacobs. Si doesn't need credit from me, he gets it on every Bob Hope Special. But it was fun working with him again. I appreciated all his help, and someday I may be able to use those jokes for our troops overseas.

Those four young blondes who look good enough to be models really are models. Their names are Shari Sveningson, Tamara Carrera, Nicole McDermott and Amber Van Lent, and I thank them for being in those pictures with me. Unfortunately, that's all I have to thank them for.

Jack Langdon has been making my life easier for thirty-five years. Typing things like this book is the least of it. He guards my time without offending people who, with the best of intentions, may want too much of it. I'll never let Jack go. How could I? He's the only one who knows where he's filed everything away.

Then there's Conrad. I've talked enough about him already. But I did neglect to mention his whole name. Should I mention it now or should I save it for my next book? I'll mention it now. How about that? The kid's only been with me two years and his name is about to close my book. It could only happen in America. And here it is! Conrad DeMichiel!

See you at the Palladium in '96.

Alan Berliner